Standard Grade

Computing Studies

revision notes

 Kevin Thompson

ISBN 1-84372-258-5
ISBN-13 978-1-84372-258-8

Published by
Leckie & Leckie Ltd, 3rd floor, 4 Queen Street, Edinburgh, EH2 1JE
Tel: 0131 220 6831 Fax: 0131 225 9987
enquiries@leckieandleckie.co.uk   www.leckieandleckie.co.uk

Special thanks to
BRW (creative packaging), Cathy Sprent (cover design), Neil Kennedy (content review),
Pumpkin House (concept design and illustration), Tony Wayte (copy-editing),
Tara Watson (proofreading), Jane Coulter (index) and Hamish Sanderson (additional illustrations).

A CIP Catalogue record for this book is available from the British Library.

Leckie & Leckie Ltd is a division of Granada Learning Limited.

Contents

Introduction

STANDARD GRADE COMPUTING STUDIES

Your computing course consists of three main areas of study:

- Computer Applications
- Computer Systems
- Computer Programming.

You are assessed on:

- knowledge and understanding of computing facts – assessed by external examination;
- problem solving in computing situations facts – assessed by external examination;
- practical assessment – assessed by tasks in school.

What these Notes cover

These Revision Notes cover the Knowledge and Understanding that you need to know for Foundation, General and Credit level. It is impossible to cover absolutely everything but you will find that all the main topics are covered.

To help you in your preparation, the notes for Foundation and General level are in normal type (like this).

The extra Credit level work is in italics (like this) on a shaded background. Your teacher will tell you whether you need to read the Credit level notes.

Problem solving

Throughout the Computing Studies course you learn how to solve problems in situations where a computer can be used.

Practical work

Some of your practical work will involve the use of computers for your practical assessment in programming, using applications and completing a project for the Examination Board.

The rest of your practical work will help you to understand the theory of computers and to see how people solve problems using a computer.

Computing words

There are many special words used in computing. These are often referred to as computer jargon. It is important that you learn what these words mean because they exactly describe computing situations. These words will be used in examination questions and you will be expected to use them properly in your answers.

Preparation for the exam

You must make sure you start your preparation in good time – it is no use trying to do it all in the few weeks before the exam. The course can be broken down into a number of topics. You will have less to do as you get to the end of the course if you learn all the facts about each topic as you study it.

Using past examination papers for revision is good final preparation. Prepare yourself for the questions by first doing your revision. Then attempt the examination questions without looking at any notes. Finally go over the questions again, using these notes for help. Alter your answers if you think some parts are wrong or you have not given a good enough answer.

It is only your teacher who can tell you if you have answered each question properly, so ask for help!

General tips on technique

- Be well prepared! It seems obvious but no-one will pass an exam if they haven't learnt their notes. Take time beforehand to talk through any weak areas with your teacher.

- Do as many past papers as you can. The best way to prepare for any exam is to do the previous ones - the same question types come up year upon year.

- Look at marks for each question. These are a good indicator for length of answer. For 3 marks you have to mention 3 points, so a one word answer will not do. On the other hand a 1 mark question should only need a short answer.

- Read the question carefully. If it says give an example then do so! If it says explain then do so. Too many marks are lost when candidates don't do as they are asked. For example:

  | Question: | Give an example of an input device. |
  | Answer: | Keyboard |

  But:

  | Question: | Explain what is meant by an input device. |
  | Answer: | An input device is a piece of hardware which allows the user to communicate with the CPU. |

- Make your revision count. There is no point in reading a page in front of the TV if you are not taking anything in. A good self-test is to jot down 3 or 4 key words from a page and when you think you have learnt them, shut the book. Look at your key headings and see what you remember about each one. If you can't remember very much then read the page again.

- In the actual exam you can do the questions in any order so do the ones you find easy first. Once you have completed these, go back and spend time on the ones you find more difficult.

General Purpose Packages

NEED FOR GENERAL PURPOSE PACKAGES

Reasons for development

Many people wanted to use microcomputers when they became popular in the 1980s. Although the types of data being used by all these people were different, the kinds of task they wanted the computer to do were the same. These tasks included:

- typing information into the computer and then editing it;
- storing the information;
- sorting data into numerical or alphabetical order;
- doing calculations with data;
- presenting the information in neat and eye-catching ways (often incorporating graphs and pictures);
- ensuring information was up-to-date, accurate and complete.

A range of software tools was required to cater for these needs and so General Purpose Packages (GPPs) were developed.

Information flow

The world is now very dependent on information. Organisations need to access and use information quickly and easily. Those who can are more likely to be successful.

Using GPPs on a computer means that:

- information can be stored in an organised and easily-retrievable form in a database;
- figures can be processed and used to produce accounts in a spreadsheet;
- data can be represented as charts or graphs using information from a spreadsheet;
- pictures can be created in a draw or paint (graphics) package;
- a word processor can be used to generate text and also to bring together information from all of the above into one comprehensive document;
- the completed document can then be sent electronically within an office. It may also be sent to other offices around the country or even in different countries by using a modem and a communications package.

Questions

1.1 In the 1980s a range of software tools called General Purpose Packages were developed to help people with common computing tasks. Describe three tasks which people wanted a computer to perform.

1.2 Briefly describe what is done by each of the following General Purpose Packages:

a) a database;

b) a word-processor;

c) a spreadsheet.

1.3 Name the extra hardware and software which would be needed, other than that normally associated with General Purpose Packages, to send information electronically from one office to another.

COMMON FEATURES

General Purpose Packages have a number of instructions and features which are common to them all:

Applications

- **Run** or **open** starts the application (program) ready for use.

Documents

- **New** begins a new document containing no data.
- **Open** or **load** uses a document that has already been saved on backing storage (such as a disc).
- **Close** or **save** saves the document on backing storage.
- **Copy** or **Move/Cut** transfers data from one place to another. **Copy** leaves the original, **Move/Cut** deletes the original.
- **Print** sends the data to a printer to be printed out.
- **Print part** prints only part of the data (e.g. prints selected text or specified pages).
- **Printer drivers** select the software to allow a specified printer to be used to print out data. The correct driver must be selected or specified when more than one printer is available.

Data

Data to be used or stored must first be inserted, and can then be changed and used in a number of ways.

Insert data. Information (e.g. words, numbers and graphics) can be entered into the document.

Delete data. Information can be deleted (removed) from the document.

Amend data. Data in the document can be altered (e.g. changing the spelling or altering the length of a line).

Copy data. The data that has been marked or selected is copied to be used in other places.

Move data. Moves the marked or selected data to the indicated position in the document.

Change appearance

The appearance of text can be altered (e.g. changing the font or size or style of the text).

Headers and footers

Headers can be set to appear in a document at the top of every page. Footers appear at the bottom of every page. Headers or footers may contain text or graphics. They often contain automatic page numbering.

Alter Human Computer Interface parameters

The Human Computer Interface (HCI) parameters govern how you use the computer system to look at and change the data and control programs. For example, you can alter the size of a window if you want to see more than one document at once, or arrange windows to stack or tile; the colours used to display selected text may need to be altered; you may want to turn up the volume for a warning sound if you make a mistake. These features are part of the way in which you work with the computer and they can be adjusted to suit your requirements.

Storage

All computers can store data. It is always a wise precaution to have more than one copy of data, regardless of the type of data stored. This means that if the original becomes lost or damaged, either accidentally or deliberately, then there is always a second copy available. Keeping regular copies like this is known as **backup**.

Standard file formats

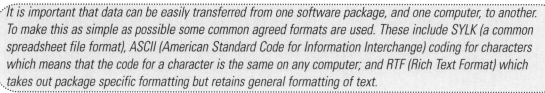

It is important that data can be easily transferred from one software package, and one computer, to another. To make this as simple as possible some common agreed formats are used. These include SYLK (a common spreadsheet file format), ASCII (American Standard Code for Information Interchange) coding for characters which means that the code for a character is the same on any computer; and RTF (Rich Text Format) which takes out package specific formatting but retains general formatting of text.

Data types

Different types of data can be stored in GPPs. These are:

Numeric. Numbers often need to be stored for calculation purposes in databases and spreadsheets. Some examples are:

> −2.34
> 4500
> 0.0004
> 23

Textual. Any characters which are not numbers, or are numbers which are not going to be used for calculations can be stored as text. Text can be alphabetic, where only letters are included, or alphanumeric which is a mixture of letters and numbers. Some examples are:

> John Smith
> 43 High Street
> £32.45
> sixty two

Graphic. Information can also be stored as graphics in word processor documents, draw or paint packages or as charts within a spreadsheet. Some examples are:

Audio. MP3s and other sound clips can be stored and used as signals, for example if a mistake is made, or to accompany presentations.

Photographic. Photographic images, from scanned images or a digital camera can be stored to be added into documents.

Animation. *Sequences of graphics which apparently move such as games characters.*

Video. *Video clips can be recorded from TV, or downloaded from digital video cameras and then edited.*

Questions

1.4 A number of processes can be carried out by all General Purpose Packages. One process to do with handling documents is starting up a new document. This creates a new blank document of the application with no data entered. Explain what happens in each of the following processes:

a) Open;

b) Print part;

c) Amend data;

d) Copy data;

e) Move data.

1.5 A process that is common to textual data in all General Purpose Packages is to change the appearance of the text. Describe some of the features of text that can be changed in this way.

1.6 a) What name is given to the process of regularly making a copy of the data produced by a General Purpose Package?

b) Explain why it is important to make a copy of your data in this way.

1.7 Describe the purpose of a printer driver.

1.8 Explain the terms header and footer and give an example of the sort of data which they might contain.

1.9 Name five different types of data which can be stored in General Purpose Packages and give one example for each type.

HUMAN COMPUTER INTERFACE

The term Human Computer Interface is usually shortened to HCI.

User-friendliness

The HCI affects how easy it is to use a program. It is the connection between the user and the computer. It is important to make computers as easy as possible for people to use, in other words to make them user-friendly. Most modern HCIs are Graphic User Interfaces or GUIs.

Menu Driven programs give the user a list of choices and an option must be selected from that list. The choices are often given as numbers.

For example:

Main Menu

1 Open document
2 Create new document
3 Print document
4 Delete document
5 Exit menu

Command Driven programs are slightly less user-friendly than menu driven ones but are often preferred by experienced users. Instead of choosing from a given list each time, the user enters command words in a special language.

For example:

Enter command:
SEARCH NAME = 'SMITH'

blank

WIMP

WIMP stands for Windows, Icons, Mouse and Pull-down menus (or Menus and Pointer). This is the kind of user interface offered by many modern computers. It is also known as a Graphical User Interface or GUI.

Wastebasket

Icons are small pictures on the screen. They are used to represent items such as floppy discs, applications and files, and the wastebasket (for deleting files).

The user often communicates with the computer by using a mouse.

The pointer is the arrow which the user controls with the mouse. It is used to point to items which are to be copied, opened, deleted or moved around the computer screen. A button on the mouse can then be pressed to use the object selected by the pointer.

The keyboard is used when numbers and letters are needed.

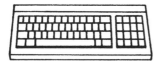

More about WIMPS

The pull-down menus and windows are the most familiar features of modern computers. Pull-down menus allow many choices to be readily available to the user without cluttering up the screen.

Windows allow text and graphics to be moved around the screen and even hidden behind other windows. This does not delete them. When the window is eventually uncovered, or moved to the front, the original data is still there. This allows several documents or applications to be open at once.

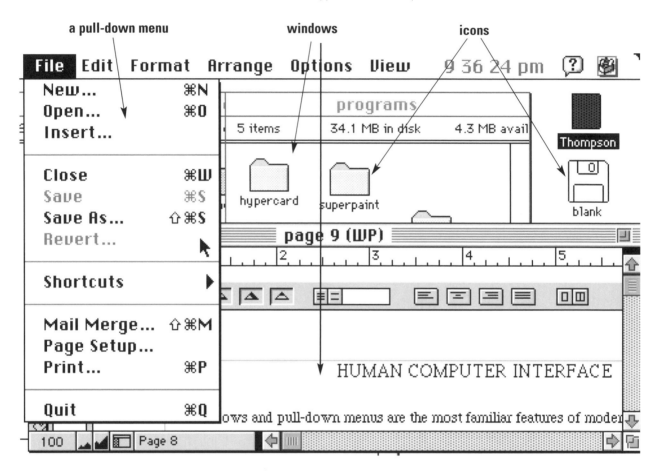

Online Tutorials and Online Help

A good HCI offers online tutorials and online help. The **tutorial** takes you step-by-step through the program demonstrating its features.

Online help is often available as a pull-down menu or a hot-key (where a special key combination acts as a command) option, which will then give a further choice of commands for which help is offered. It can be accessed while the program is in use.

Save

The Save command allows files to be written to disc for access at a later date. It is activated by choosing Save from the File menu or by using the appropriate key combination.

Template

A template is a commonly used document outline supplied by a software manufacturer e.g. a word processor may give document templates for: Brochure, directory, manual, and thesis. The user can also add templates of their own.

Wizard

A wizard is a piece of software that takes the user step-by-step through a task. They can be used within a variety of different packages – a wizard to set up email details, a wizard to set up a mail merge.

Keyboard shortcuts

Although features in most modern packages are accessed through the toolbar and pull-down menus at the top many experienced users prefer to use keyboard shortcuts. This is where a combination of keys are used to issue a command. For example, Ctrl P (hold down the Ctrl key while pressing the P key) means PRINT, Ctrl O (hold down the Ctrl key while pressing the O key) means OPEN. (On an Applemac computer the Apple key is used instead of Ctrl.)

Customising HCI

Some packages and indeed some computers allow the user to customize the HCI to their own preferences e.g. on a PC a theme may be chosen for background, alert sounds, icons.

Questions

1.10   a)   Explain the term Human Computer Interface.

          b)   Name two examples of features of the Human Computer Interface which can be altered by the user.

1.11   A good Human Computer Interface is said to be user-friendly. Explain what this means.

1.12   Some programs are menu-driven and others are command-driven.

          a)   Which type of program is said to be more user-friendly?

          b)   Which type of program is usually preferred by more experienced users?

          c)   Describe how the user might select what to do next when using a command-driven program.

          d)   Describe how the user might select what to do next when using a menu-driven program.

1.13   Many modern computers use a WIMP system for the user to communicate with the computer.

    a) Explain the meaning of the term WIMP.

    b) Give an alternative name for a WIMP interface.

    c) Explain what the keyboard is used for in a WIMP system.

1.14   a) What is an icon?

    b) Give two examples of icons.

    c) Describe how a user might select an icon in a WIMP system.

1.15   Briefly describe the difference between an online tutorial and online help.

WORD-PROCESSING

A word processor allows you to enter, amend, delete, save, retrieve and print text.

Enter the text can be typed in.

Amend the text can be altered.

Delete the text can be removed altogether.

Save the text can be saved on backing storage (disc).

Retrieve the text can be loaded back into the memory of the computer.

Print the text can be printed out on a printer.

Wordwrap

A word may not fit into the space that is left when you get near the end of a line of typing. The wordwrap feature means that whole word will automatically be carried to the start of the new line when you get to the end of a line of typing.

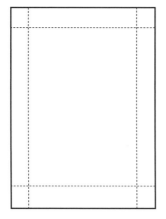

Page size

The size of pages in a document can be altered. These options allow different sizes of paper to be used. The amount of text on a page may also be altered by setting margins at top, bottom, left and right.

Tabulation

Every computer keyboard has a TAB key. When this is pressed, the cursor (usually a flashing line in your text showing where the next character will be printed) is moved to the right to the next TAB position. You can place the tab settings in the positions you prefer, or use the tabs preset by the word processor. These are often set at every 1.27 cm (or half inch).

Checking your spelling

Almost all modern word-processing systems allow you to check your spelling. A separate file contains all the words that the system knows (typically 50 000 or more). Each word is compared with this dictionary file when you choose to check the spelling. Any words not found are marked in some way; possible replacements are often offered. There will, of course, be many words that the system does not know, such as names of people or towns. The system can usually learn new words by adding them to its dictionary file.

Alignment

Modern word-processing systems allow several kinds of text justification. Left justified text is always lined up on the left-hand side of the page; right justified text is lined up on the right-hand side of the page; centre justified text is equally spaced to each side of the centre of the page; fully justified text has extra spaces added between the words on each line so that the left-hand and right-hand sides are both lined up.

Standard paragraphs

Standard paragraphs are of value when the same text is used over and over again in many different documents. If you were sending out letters for a company you might have one saying there will be a delay on an order. This would **not** be typed every time but stored on a disc and loaded into the word processor when needed. Different paragraphs can be loaded in and mixed and matched until the desired letter is formed.

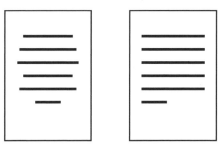

Dear Sir

We regret to inform you that the item you requested is not in stock at present.

We have requested it from our supplier and it will be with you within the next 10 days.

We apologise for the delay and assure you of our best attention at all times.

Yours faithfully

Joseph Smith
Managing Director

Tables

Tables may be used to format data neatly.

Local Authority	Number of secondary schools	Number of primary schools
Edinburgh	23	102
Glasgow	30	198
Dundee	10	41
Stirling	7	43
Aberdeen	12	57

Tables can then be resized by adding extra rows or columns.

Local Authority	Number of secondary schools	Number of primary schools	Number of secondary pupils	Number of primary pupils
Edinburgh	23	102	20116	27856
Glasgow	30	198	29803	43572
Dundee	10	41	8664	10990
Stirling	7	43	5807	7020
Aberdeen	12	57	10628	14082
Highland	29	185	14749	18190

Page Breaks

Artificial Page Breaks may be inserted to force the document to take a new page before it would normally do so such as when starting a new section in a long document.

Search and Replace

The Search and Replace function allows you to look for a word or phrase within a document and replace it with a different word or phrase automatically. Imagine you had written a letter to a Mr Smith and wanted the same letter to go to Mr Jones. On a typewriter you would have had to retype the whole letter. The word processor will replace every occurrence of Smith with Jones.

Dear Mr Smith

Thank you very much for your interest in employment at Wanda.

However, we regret to inform you that your application has been unsuccessful.

We wish you success in your search for employment.

Dear Mr Jones

Thank you very much for your interest in employment at Wanda.

However, we regret to inform you that your application has been unsuccessful.

We wish you success in your search for employment.

Standard letters and Mail Merge

A standard letter is one which is sent to many people with only a few details (such as name and address) changed for each person.

The word processed letter is linked to either a database file or another word processor file which contains the details to be changed each time. These personal details are then merged in as each letter is printed making each one look unique.

You can send personalised letters to many thousands of people this way. This process is called mail merge. Much of the 'junk mail' which people receive is produced using standard letters

For example, a standard letter might look like:

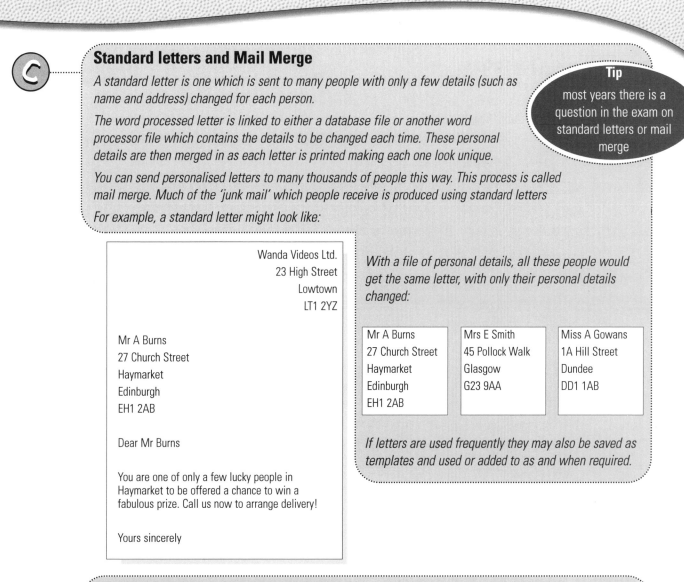

Wanda Videos Ltd.
23 High Street
Lowtown
LT1 2YZ

Mr A Burns
27 Church Street
Haymarket
Edinburgh
EH1 2AB

Dear Mr Burns

You are one of only a few lucky people in Haymarket to be offered a chance to win a fabulous prize. Call us now to arrange delivery!

Yours sincerely

With a file of personal details, all these people would get the same letter, with only their personal details changed:

Mr A Burns	Mrs E Smith	Miss A Gowans
27 Church Street	45 Pollock Walk	1A Hill Street
Haymarket	Glasgow	Dundee
Edinburgh	G23 9AA	DD1 1AB
EH1 2AB		

If letters are used frequently they may also be saved as templates and used or added to as and when required.

Optical Character Recognition (OCR)

It is now possible to scan a document which has been previously typed or word processed and using a special software technique called Optical Character Recognition (OCR) to treat it as if it had been typed in, allowing it to be edited.

Speech Input

Modern computers also allow speech input using special software and a microphone. This has to be trained to a particular voice which takes some time but is then fairly accurate. Some professionals now use them instead of employing secretaries. They are also of great benefit to special needs people who may have difficulty typing.

Questions

1.16 A word-processor allows the user to enter, amend, delete, save, retrieve and print out text. Briefly describe what is meant by each of the highlighted terms.

1.17 Explain the term wordwrap and state why it is often used by word-processors.

1.18 a) Explain the term tabulation.

b) What are the typical preset TAB settings in a word-processing system?

c) Describe what the cursor might look like when using a word-processor.

1.19 a) A name and address on a letter might be right justified/aligned. Explain why you might want to right justify the name and address and draw a diagram to show what the text would look like.

b) The text in a book might be left justified/aligned. Explain why you might want to left justify the text and draw a diagram to show what the text would look like.

c) The columns in a newspaper might be fully justified/aligned. Explain why you might want to fully justify the columns and draw a diagram to show what the text would look like.

1.20 A spellcheck system allows the spelling of all the words in a word-processed document to be checked.

a) Where are all the words recognised by the system usually kept?

b) How many words does a typical system recognise?

c) What sort of words would the system probably NOT recognise?

d) How does the system learn new words?

1.21 a) What is a standard paragraph?

b) Give an example of a situation where standard paragraphs could be used.

1.22 a) What is a standard letter?

b) The letter, produced on a word-processor, can be linked to another type of file. Name the type of file.

c) What name is given to the process of producing standard letters by combining the word-processed information with that stored on the other type of file?

SPREADSHEETS

What is a spreadsheet?

A spreadsheet is an electronic table or grid made up of cells arranged in rows and columns. Each cell is named from the column and row which it occupies:

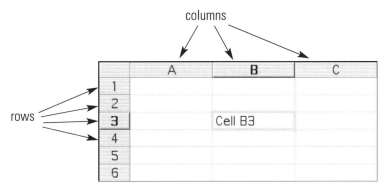

Values, text and formulae

A cell can contain one of three things:

- A value or number e.g. 47, 132, 3.6

- Text e.g. Monday, Total, Average

- A formula, which may be simple, such as:

      B5 + C5,   D4*E4,   SUM(C5:C10)

  or more complex, such as:

      B5*(B6 + B7*B8) - (B9 + B10)

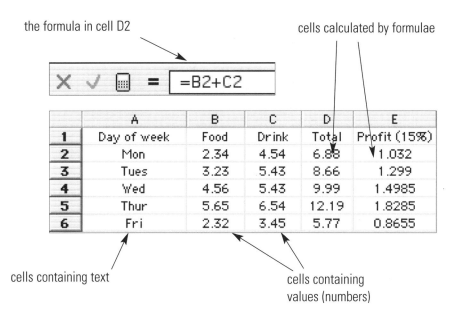

Functions

Spreadsheets can use **Functions** for carrying out calculations. These are built-in formulae shown by a simple word e.g. AVERAGE(first cell-last cell…) (which calculates the average value of the data from the first cell to the last cell) MINIMUM(…) and MAXIMUM(…).(which calculate the minimum value and maximum value of the data from the first cell to the last cell) These functions all return one value. (Note that in some software Min and Max are used.)

If these functions were applied to the following we would find:

	A	B	C	D	E	F	G
1		test1	test2	test3	AVERAGE (B+C+D)/3	MINIMUM (smallest)	MAXIMUM (biggest)
2	Ryan	3	5	13	7	3	13
3	Michael	10	15	32	19	10	32
4	Lesley	1	2	3	2	1	3
5	Christopher	40	50	60	50	40	60
6	Christy	70	80	90	80	70	90

Note the formula in cell E2 is the function AVERAGE(B2;D2). In other words, the AVERAGE function calculates the average value of the numbers in cells B2, C2 and D2.

F2 is the function MIN(B2;D2)

G2 is the function MAX(B2;D2)

Charting

Most modern spreadsheets allow you to produce charts directly from the spreadsheet values. The user may choose from several types of chart, including a pie chart, a bar chart, or a line graph.

For example:

- **The spreadsheet:**

	A	B	C	D	E
1	Day of week	Food	Drink	Total	Profit (15%)
2	Mon	2.34	4.54	6.88	1.032
3	Tues	3.23	5.43	8.66	1.299
4	Wed	4.56	5.43	9.99	1.4985
5	Thur	5.65	6.54	12.19	1.8285
6	Fri	2.32	3.45	5.77	0.8655

- **The bar chart:**

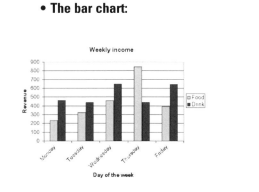

- **The pie chart:**

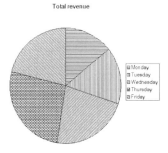

- **The line graph:**

Calculations

Spreadsheets can be set to calculate values either as soon as a formula is entered (this is known as **automatic calculation**) or only when told to do so (this is known as **manual calculation**).

Normally, most people use the default option which is automatic calculation. However, if large numbers of formulae are to be entered or the calculations are very complicated, it is usually quicker to switch automatic calculation off.

Inserting and changing size

Extra rows (1, 2, 3, ...) and columns (A, B, C, ...) may be added to an existing spreadsheet if required. It is also possible to alter the width of columns and, in some spreadsheets, the row height.

	A	B
1	normal height	
2	double height	

Replication

Similar formulae are often needed in a range of cells. Rather than type in the same formulae many times, it can be quicker to use **replication**. The contents of one cell are copied into another and the formulae automatically adjust for the new row or column.

	A	B	C
1			=A1*B1
2			=A2*B2
3			=A3*B3
4			=A4*B4
5			=A5*B5

The formula to multiply the cells in each column has been replicated down column C.

Attributes

Numbers to be used in calculations in a spreadsheet must be typed in **only** as numbers. In other words, the cells must contain no text (e.g. no £, %, $ etc). They can, however, be displayed in different ways by altering the attributes (or display options) of a cell.

For example, the number 2.987 could be shown as:

```
2.987
3
2.99 or
£2.99
```

depending on the option chosen.

In the same way, dates can be displayed in different formats.

For example:

```
12/2/05

February 12, 2005

Sat, February 12, 2005
```

In some spreadsheets, this option also allows you to alter the style of text using features such as **bold**, underlined and *italics* and the position in the cell where the text is displayed, making it left, centre, or right justified.

	A	B	C
1	**bold**	underlined	*italics*
2	left	centre	right

Formulae involving conditions

More complex spreadsheet formulae can involve conditions. This means that a cell will take on one value if a certain condition is true and a different value if it is false.

B1=IF(A1>69;1;2)

	A	B
1	72	1
2	43	2

This formula means that if A1 contains a number greater than 69 then B1 = 1 (A1>69 is true).
If A1 is NOT greater than 69 then B1 = 2 (A1>69 is false).

Tip
most years there is a question in the exam on a formula using the IF condition

Relative cell references

You saw earlier that replication means copying from one cell to a group of others. When this happens, you normally want the cell references to change according to the row and column they are copied into.

Examine the following:

	A	B	C
1			=A1*B1
2			=A2*B2
3			=A3*B3
4			=A4*B4
5			=A5*B5

This is the replication example from the previous page. Note that the row numbers for both A and B change as you look down column C. This is the normal replication procedure and all cell references are said to be relative.

This is not always the case, however, and there is a way to keep a cell reference constant. In this case the reference is said to be absolute.

Absolute cell references

In the example below, it is important that the reference to cell A2 stays constant throughout the replication since it is only A2 which contains 17.5%. In this spreadsheet, this is achieved by using a $ sign before each part of the cell reference. Replicating cell A2 is an example of absolute replication.

Tip
there is often a question in the exam on relative and absolute replication

	A	B	C
1	VAT =		=$A$2*B1
2	17.5%		=$A$2*B2
3			=$A$2*B3
4			=$A$2*B4
5			=$A$2*B5

Cell protection

A spreadsheet is usually set up by one person, but many others may make use of it. In an attempt to minimise the danger of inexperienced users changing areas of the spreadsheet accidentally, cells are often locked or protected after information has been placed in them. These cells, of course, have to be unlocked before they can be altered. Cells containing labels or formulae are usually protected.

	A	B	C
1	Overtime	Hours	Hours
2	Sheet	Basic	Overtime
3	Mon	40	5
4	Tues	35	10
5	Wed	37	12
6	Thur	40	7
7	Fri	40	5
8	Sat	42	6

Cells A1 to A8, B1, B2, C1 and C2 would be locked since the information which they contain will be the same every week. The other cells contain information which will change weekly and so will be left unprotected.

Questions

1.23 Briefly describe the appearance of a typical spreadsheet.

1.24 Name the three different types of information that a spreadsheet can contain. Give an example to illustrate each type of information.

1.25 Name two types of chart that can be drawn using the data in a spreadsheet and draw a diagram to show the appearance of each one.

1.26 a) Explain the difference between automatic calculation and manual calculation when referring to the use of a formula in a spreadsheet.

b) Describe one situation where it would be preferable to use manual calculation and explain why it is preferable.

c) Which option is usually the default?

1.27 A spreadsheet is set up to contain the formula shown here in cell C1. Explain what is meant by the term replication and use the spreadsheet to show the effect of replication of the formula shown in cell C1 down column C.

	A	B	C
1			=A1+B1
2			
3			
4			
5			
6			
7			
8			

1.28 a) Explain what is meant by the term cell attributes and describe the effect that altering the attributes would have on a number stored in a spreadsheet cell.

b) Describe the effect that changing attributes could have on the date for the first day of January in the year 2000 stored in a spreadsheet cell.

1.29 A function is a complex formula which returns a single value. State what value each of the following functions would give:

a) AVERAGE(..)

b) MINIMUM(..)

c) MAXIMUM(..)

1.30 Cell protection is sometimes used to lock parts of a spreadsheet.

a) What kinds of information should be locked on a spreadsheet?

b) Why might it be desirable to lock these cells?

1.31 *The following formula is stored in a spreadsheet cell: B1=IF(A1>31;0;1). Explain the meaning of this formula.*

1.32 *When the contents of a cell are replicated the process could be absolute or relative.*

a) Give examples to illustrate the terms relative replication and absolute replication.

b) Name one way in which the spreadsheet can be instructed to make a reference to a cell absolute.

c) Describe one situation where the user might want to make a reference to a cell absolute.

DATABASES

A database is an organised collection of data. The organization allows for easy retrieval. This is true whether the data is stored on paper or in a computer.

Files, records and fields

Before computers were used for databases, data was held on record cards, collected in **files**. The file would contain many cards with the same type of information on them.

Each card is a **record**.

Each category of information is a **field**.

For example:

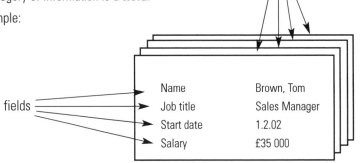

Computerised information

A database program controls a database on a computer. The data is organised as shown above into files, records and fields.

Create new files begins a new database file containing no information. For example, a new file called Company Employees might have fields, but until data is entered, it contains no records:

Fields	Record
Name	
Job title	
Start date	
Salary	

Each employee will have a record with their unique information in the appropriate fields:

Fields	Record
Name	Brown, Tom
Job title	Sales Manager
Start date	1.2.02
Salary	£35 000

Fields	Record
Name	Smith, Wendy
Job title	Personnel Manager
Start date	3.12.00
Salary	£40 000

Edit record allows individual items of information to be changed. Imagine Wendy Smith got married to Tom Brown. Her name would be changed to Wendy Brown. So it would need changed on the database record.

Fields	Record
Name	Brown, Wendy
Job title	Personnel Manager
Start date	3.12.00
Salary	£40 000

Add new records allows new records to be added to the database. For example, when new employees arrive, their details are entered onto blank records.

Fields	Record
Name	Greig, Jean
Job title	Secretary
Start date	11.11.03
Salary	£15 000

Adding new fields allows extra information to be added to each record in the database. This means adding a new field. For example, a new field can be entered to record the registration number of all company car drivers:

Fields	Record
Name	Brown, Tom
Job title	Sales Manager
Start date	1.2.02
Salary	£35 000
Car Reg	J123 RSL

Fields	Record
Name	Smith, Wendy
Job title	Personnel Manager
Start date	3.12.00
Salary	£40 000
Car Reg	L354 QWY

The new field would be added to all the records.

Fields can be of specific types

Field name	Field contents	Field type
Name	Tom Brown	Text
Start Date	1.2.02	Date
Age	36	Number
Shift start	09:00	Time
Photo		Graphic

Searching

A computerised database program can search through a file very rapidly to find a certain record. There are two kinds of searches:

- **simple searches** check only one field;
- **complex searches** check two or more fields.

In the above examples, a simple search would be where Salary was greater than £20 000.

A more complex search might be Salary greater than £20 000 AND Start Date before 1.1.03.

Often CD ROMs now contain huge databases such as encyclopedias or even phone books. They can have a simple template which the user fills in to show what they are searching for:

Enter title	Computer Studies
Enter author	Thompson
Enter publisher	Leckie and Leckie

In more complex searches you can choose to INCLUDE or EXCLUDE certain records to keep a search more limited:

Topic	George
Include	III
Exclude	Dragon

In this example we are looking for any reference to George but it must also contain III so George V would not be returned. It specifically excludes Dragon so any references to George and the Dragon would also be left out. These are Keyword searches.

Note: a search engine is a piece of software allowing the WWW to be searched

Altering record format

It is possible to display databases in different ways. Sometimes it is better to see all the data as a card layout. For other purposes it is more useful to see the database organised into columns.

For example:

- Card format:

Fields	**Record**
Name	Brown, Tom
Job title	Sales Manager
Start date	1.2.02
Salary	£35 000

Fields	Record
Name	Smith, Wendy
Job title	Personnel Manager
Start date	3.12.00
Salary	£40 000

Fields	Record
Name	Greig, Jean
Job title	Secretary
Start date	11.11.03
Salary	£15 000

- List or Table format:

Name	Job title	Start date	Salary
Brown, Tom	Sales Manager	1.2.02	£35000
Smith, Wendy	Personnel Manager	3.12.00	£40000
Greig, Jean	Secretary	11.11.03	£15000

Sometimes different views of data showing only selected fields are useful (imagine a database with fifty fields but you are only interested in 2 or 3 of them):

Name	Job title	Salary
Brown, Tom	Sales Manager	£35000
Smith, Wendy	Personnel Manager	£40000
Greig, Jean	Secretary	£15000

Sorting

As well as searching files on a particular field, it is also possible to sort files into an order of your choice.

- Sorted by Salary: lowest to highest

Name	Start date	Salary
Greig, Jean	11.11.03	£15000
Brown, Tom	1.2.02	£35000
Smith, Wendy	3.12.00	£40000

- Sorted by Name:

Name	Start date	Salary
Brown, Tom	1.2.02	£35000
Greig, Jean	11.11.03	£15000
Smith, Wendy	3.12.00	£40000

• Sorted by Start Date:

Name	Start date	Salary
Smith, Wendy	3.12.00	£40000
Brown, Tom	1.2.02	£35000
Greig, Jean	11.11.03	£15000

Sorting on two fields

In addition to sorting a database on one field, it is sometimes useful to have two-field sorts. One field is given precedence and only if the entries in it are the same for two or more records, does the second field become involved.

Tip
there is often a question in the exam on two-field search or two-field sort

Imagine sorting into alphabetical order a list of 1000 names organised as forenames and surnames. The surname SMITH is likely to come up more than once, so the forename would then be used as a second field. This would mean that all the Alan Smiths would come before the John Smiths and so on.

Computed fields

*Some database programs allow the use of computed fields. The contents of these are worked out by the computer rather than inserted by the user. If a field in the database contained **Date of Birth**, then a possible computed field would be **Age**. This would be calculated by entering a formula, such as:*

Tip
most years there is a question in the exam on computed fields

Current Date – Date of Birth.

Input and output format

The user can alter the format of the input screen to make it easier to enter data. For some databases, it is easier to enter all of one field before moving onto the next. For others, an entire record (card) of information would be better entered at one time. Similarly, the format of the output from a database can also be customised by the user. This is achieved by creating a report containing the information that is required. A report may contain only a few fields from a database. It may also contain headers, footers and page numbers similar to those in a word processed document. The report may also contain extra information not available at record level, such as adding together the contents of a particular field for all the records.

Questions

1.33 A database stored on disc contains the names of ten friends, with their dates of birth and favourite colour. Give an example from this to explain each of the terms file, record and field.

1.34 One operation that can be carried out on a database is searching. The search can be simple or it can be complex. Explain what happens when a file is searched and describe the difference between a simple search and a complex search.

1.35 The information in a database can be displayed in different ways.

a) Give a name which describes one particular way in which a file is displayed.

b) Name two ways in which database information is commonly displayed.

1.36 a) A field in a database can be computed. Explain what this means.

b) What is the advantage to the user in being able to change the input format for data?

c) What may happen when the format of output from a database is changed?

1.37 a) Explain what happens when a database is sorted according to the contents of one field.

b) Give an example to show the advantage of sorting a database on two fields.

GRAPHICS

A graphics program allows you to combine pictures and text in many different ways.

You can:

- Draw graphics e.g. design a picture for a business card.
- Add text (words) to your graphic

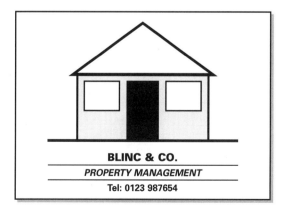

Change tools

Select different tools to add parts of the drawing (e.g. draw lines, circles and rectangles).

Change attributes

Alter tool attributes (e.g. change the width of a line, the fill pattern of an object or the style of some text).

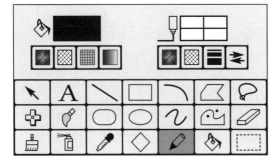

Scale the graphic

Change the size of the graphic by making it larger or smaller.

Rotate the graphic

Turn the whole graphic through a certain number of degrees.

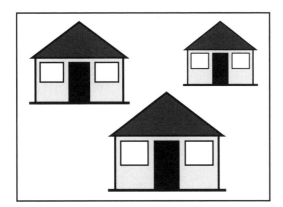

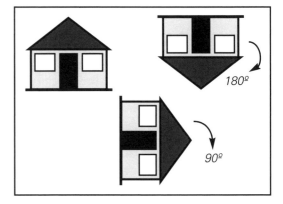

Scan and edit the graphic

Graphics may be scanned in if they are not available in electronic format. For example, a user could draw something and then scan it and edit it.

Crop the Graphic

Graphics may also be cropped to remove excess unwanted parts or simply to resize them.

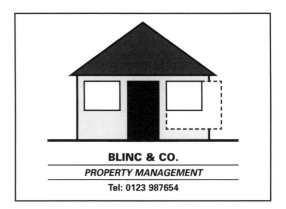

Questions

I.38 a) Describe three tools which you may expect to find in a graphics program.

b) What are tool attributes?

c) Give two examples of the effect of changing tool attributes.

d) What happens when a graphic is scaled?

EXPERT SYSTEMS

Expert Systems or Knowledge Systems

An Expert System (or Knowledge System) is a system or program which can imitate some of the functions of a human expert in a small area of expertise. They address problems normally thought to require human specialists for their solution. Some of the areas covered by Expert Systems are:

- giving legal advice (helping lawyers)
- medical diagnosis (helping doctors)
- car diagnosis (helping mechanics)

For example:

```
IF plugs won't spark      AND
car has fuel              AND
battery is charged        THEN
ADVICE is ignition fault
```

Advantages of Expert Systems

Expert systems allow us to keep, reproduce or share, expertise that is in short supply and is difficult or expensive to obtain. They also allow the release of the human expert from routine or boring tasks to allow them to concentrate on more difficult issues and on training and research.

Social Legal and Ethical Issues

There are a range of other considerations when using Expert Systems. On a legal front, who has ownership of the knowledge and who would be to blame if a medical program made a wrong diagnosis. Likewise some people find it difficult to deal with and trust a machine rather than a human being.

Questions

I.39 a) What is an Expert System (also called a Knowledge System)?

b) Name two areas covered by Knowledge Systems and give the occupations of people who would use them in that way.

ELECTRONIC COMMUNICATION AND NETWORKS

People working with GPPs may want to share with others the files they have created. This often involves some form of electronic communication. There are many different methods of electronic communication.

Networks

When a number of computers are connected together by cabling, they are said to be on a network. The users can now share files and expensive peripherals, such as printers and modems. The two main types of network are LANs and WANs.

LANs (Local Area Networks)

A group of computers connected by cables and all in one building is known as a LAN or Local Area Network.

There are various types of network cabling and software. Almost all of these allow very fast data transfer with very few errors. Increasingly today wireless networks are used (such as Apple's Airport©) where no cabling is required. This allows greater flexibility in putting computers where they are needed rather than where the cables are.

Local Area Networks are used to connect computers and other devices in the same room, computers in different rooms and even computers on different floors thus allowing sharing of data and peripherals such as printers or scanners. The cabling is relatively inexpensive. The main cables for computers use twisted wires. Special optical fibre cables are used over longer distances.

WANs (Wide Area Networks)

Groups of computers linked together over larger distances are known as WANs or Wide Area Networks.

Computers connected in this way can be in different towns, countries or continents. They can be joined via the telephone system using **modems** (modulator/demodulators) which change the computer signal into a telephone signal and back again.

The Internet is a very important WAN used by many millions of people worldwide.

Electronic Mail (email)

One of the most popular uses of networks is for sending electronic mail. Users with the correct equipment (a computer, a network connection and communications software) can subscribe to an email service. This is a large computer system which sets up areas of memory as electronic mailboxes, each allocated to a different person. Each owner of a mailbox can connect at any time to see if any messages are in his mailbox and can send messages to any other mailbox holder.

Advantages

Messages are sent instantly and may be sent to whole groups of people at one time.

Disadvantages

Only people who have network connections and who subscribe to the service can send and receive mail.

Netiquette

This is a new term which describes good behaviour in emails and online generally. For example, one rule is not to use BLOCK CAPITALS since this is considered to be like shouting. It helps to remember there is a human being at the other end of your communication – not just a computer.

Text messaging

Nowadays almost everyone has a mobile phone thus enabling a new form of communication – text messaging. This is a cheap and fast way to stay in touch by typing short messages into your mobile phone and sending them to others. It even has its own language with many abbreviations being used. Can you read the message on the left?

File Transfer

It is possible to send a file such as a business card or a picture from one user to another. This can be done by mobile phone or by using a computer. Files are often sent as attachments to emails: documents and graphics can be sent this way.

Security Issues

It is important that only authorized users can access a network in say a large company. And that data sent between computers is safe from prying eyes.

This is done by a variety of techniques including use of passwords, physical locks on computer systems and encryption where messages are sent in a coded format. This last technique is important for sending details such as credit card numbers to companies.

On- and offline

Online means under the control of the processor. Conversely, offline means not under processor control. Some associated terms are:

- Online help means help that is available from within a program, usually from a pull-down menu or by pressing a special function key.
- Online tutorials are programs which teach you how to use packages. A separate program leads you through the steps required.

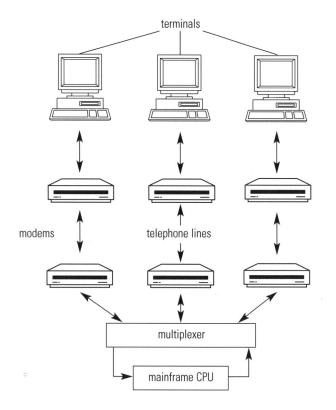

terminals

modems   telephone lines

Multi-access

In a multi-access system, a mainframe computer can be accessed by many users at one time. Each user has a terminal usually with little processing power, consisting of a keyboard and screen. These can either be near the mainframe itself and connected by cables or be some considerable distance away making use of modems. In this latter case they are known as remote terminals.

Each terminal is connected to the mainframe through a piece of hardware called a multiplexer. This allows the operating system to give short bursts of processor time to each terminal in turn (called 'time slicing') so that each terminal is apparently the sole user of the system.

For example, many bank customers may use the same main computer, which they access from 'hole in the wall' cash terminals. This allows a customer to check his or her balance (for example, held in Edinburgh) whether he or she logs on in London or John o' Groats. Each customer appears to be the only user but in reality there may be hundreds online at the same time.

Network Interface cards

For a computer to operate on a network it needs to be fitted with a network interface card (sometimes called an Ethernet card).

Many modern computers now have these fitted as standard but they can be added quite cheaply to almost any computer.

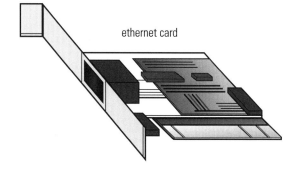

ethernet card

Clients and Servers

Computers on a network can act as Clients where they look elsewhere on the network for files and software or Servers (these usually have bigger hard drives fitted) when they supply the software and/or files to others on the network.

Questions

1.40 a) A computer can be connected to a network. What is a network and what advantages does it have over computers that are not networked?

b) Name the two main types of network and compare them on the basis of the distances involved, the cable system used and the number of transmission errors that occur.

1.41 a) What is needed for someone to be able to use electronic mail?

b) What is an electronic mailbox?

c) Give one advantage and one disadvantage of electronic mail.

1.42 What is meant by the term netiquette? Give an example of something that is considered bad netiquette.

1.43 a) *Briefly describe the main points of a multi-access system.*

b) *Explain what is meant by the term remote terminal.*

c) *Describe the process of time slicing and state what effect this has on each user of a multi-access system.*

INTERNET

Information available

The Internet offers a huge amount of information, more readily available to anyone with access than ever before. In one sense it can be viewed as one enormous database with many millions of pages of information. The Internet itself is actually a network of computer networks – many computers which are permanently linked together.

It also allows access to many services such as news reports, online shopping, online banking, airline and holiday booking.

When a user logs on to the Internet they connect to one of these computers, via an Internet Service Provider (ISP) – a firm that charges for their services.

Browser

To use the Internet most people use a special piece of software called a browser. The most common of these are Netscape Navigator® Firefox, Internet Explorer® and Safari. They allow pages from the Internet to be seen through a WIMP HCI.

Internet-ready Computer

Most computers bought today are advertised as Internet-ready. This means they have a built in modem and a choice of ISP software already installed so all the user has to do is plug them into a phone line.

World Wide Web

The most widely used part of the Internet is the World Wide Web (WWW). It is a collection of web pages. Pages on the web are written in hypertext (HTML). This is a special language which allows links to other web pages. These are called hyperlinks and are usually in blue and underlined.

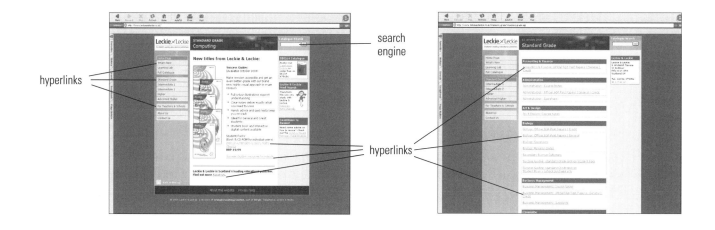

Online and offline in communications

When two computers are linked together and are able to exchange information, they are said to be **online**. There is often an online light on a modem to show that the telephone connection has not been broken. When one or other user breaks the connection, the computers go **offline**. In Internet terms online means connected to the Internet and offline is disconnected.

Phone time costs money. Most documents are therefore prepared offline. The connection is then made and the document is sent from one computer to the other. The users then log off and the computers become off-line once more.

Dial-up and Broadband

The Internet can be accessed from anywhere provided there is a standard telephone connection to plug the modem into. This is called a dial-up connection.

Many users now have a broadband connection meaning they are permanently connected to the Internet, at speeds of 10 – 160 times faster than a dial-up line.

Search Engines

Since the Internet is so vast it is very difficult to actually find the information the user wants. There is no index! Instead people use **a search engine**. This is a piece of software that allows you to type in what you want and brings back suggested pages for you to look at. Some popular search engines are Ask Jeeves®, Google®, Altavista®, Yahoo®, Lycos® and Hotbot®.

More about Search Engines

*It is possible to do more advanced searches with most search engines. This is necessary because many searches bring back too many results! For example, if the word **computer** is typed into Yahoo® it finds 262,000,000 matches! - obviously too many to look at. By choosing advanced options most search engines allow you to look for exact phrases or to give excluded words. Changing the search to **computer words** matches only 7,550 and **definition of computer words** matches only 2.*

Download software

The Internet is a great source of computer software and often it is possible to download this directly to your own machine. This means the program transfers from a computer somewhere else in the world (you don't even need to know where) directly onto your own computer desktop.

Software types

Downloaded software is generally one of three types. It can be:

- ***freeware** – which means anyone can use it at no charge,*

- ***shareware** – which means you usually have a free trial of a month or so and then pay a small fee (around £15–20) to continue using it or*

- ***commercial** which often has to have a full fee paid in advance before it can be downloaded.*

Video Conferencing

*One use of the Internet that has become popular in business and education is **video conferencing**. This is where two or more people at different places in the country, or even in different countries can see and hear each other and have a conversation as if they were in the same room. Each requires specialized hardware which usually consists of two or more screens and a powerful microphone.*

Mobile Internet Technology

Mobile Internet technology became generally available in 2002/3 and will advance rapidly over the next few years. Users can access the Internet without needing a phone connection in several main ways – via mobile phone and PDA (Personal Digital Assistant). So far the phone service is limited but can give access to some web pages. The PDA is more sophisticated allowing imaging too.

Many public areas such as hotels and airports are now offering WiFi or Wireless Fidelity Internet access where a laptop fitted with a wireless card can simply login when it comes within range of the system.

Questions

1.44 Give 3 examples of online services which the Internet provides.

1.45 Special software is needed to access the World Wide Web e.g. Internet Explorer. What name is used to describe this software?

1.46 What is hypertext?

1.47 Give the name of 2 search engines in common use.

1.48 a) A device is online to the computer. What does this mean?

b) Explain why documents which are to be transmitted electronically are often prepared offline.

1.49 *Explain the difference between freeware, shareware and commercial software.*

DESKTOP PUBLISHING

A desktop publishing package allows the relatively inexperienced user to create high quality pages such as those in magazines or newsletters. They are usually a combination of a word-processing package and a graphics package although they can have other features which are not found in either of the above. Their main advantage is control over page layout. Many of the features are similar to those found in word-processing and graphics packages.

Templates and wizards

Pages may be created from nothing by the user but the more common layouts are usually given with the package as **templates**. Alternatively **wizards** may take the user step-by-step through the page creation.

Enter Text

Text may be typed in or copied and pasted from elsewhere, such as from a word-processing package.

Add Clip Art

Often large numbers of simple graphics - called clip art – are supplied with these packages and they may be placed on the page. Alternatively many thousands of clip art pictures are available on the Internet and these or graphics from other packages, may be imported.

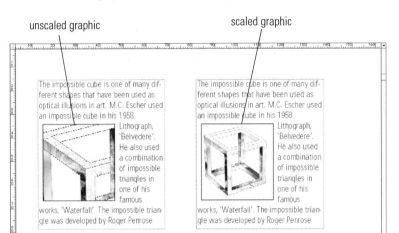

unscaled graphic   scaled graphic

Scaling Graphics

Once graphics are placed on a page they may be resized or scaled to fit the space available.

Other Features of DTP packages

Once the text and pictures are on a page they may be moved around to suit different purposes, for example in a newsletter, the user may want different numbers of columns. This is called changing the layout.

Other text sources

Text may also be scanned in using OCR software or imported from a word processor.

Text Wrap

A feature of many DTP packages is text wrap around graphics. Here the graphic is placed on the page and the text 'wraps' itself around allowing for the shape of the graphic.

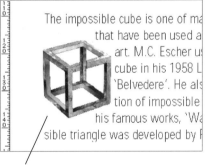

text wrapping around an image

Questions

1.50   Many packages today come with a) wizards and b) templates. Explain what is meant by these terms.

1.51   What is clip art?

1.52   What is meant by:

     a)   importing a graphic?

     b)   scaling a graphic?

PRESENTATION AND MULTIMEDIA

Multimedia refers to the use of new technology to present information. It uses computers to display textual and graphical information in an interactive environment. CD-ROMs/DVDs and laser discs are often used, in conjunction with software stored on conventional backing storage, because they can store very large amounts of data. This can be read quickly to produce high quality moving images with sound.

Presentation packages

Presentation packages such as PowerPoint or Keynote can be used for teaching or giving talks etc. They allow the user to link together a whole series of slides containing text, images, sounds and even video clips or Internet links.

Creating a presentation

Presentations can be made choosing from a series of templates which come with most packages. As with DTP packages wizards are also often used to lead the user through a simple set-up. Users can also start from a blank page to create their own template.

Enter Text

Text may be typed in or copied and pasted from elsewhere.

Add Graphic

Graphics may be added from within the package itself or collected elsewhere (e.g. from the Internet) and added in.

Linking slides and screens

Individual pages or slides may be linked together in any order the user wishes.

Assembling Pages

It is possible to have pages appear in their entirety or one piece at a time. Special effects can also be used to show a page building up in front of the viewer to a sound or animated accompaniment.

Audio clips

Audio can be added either from within the program itself or from clips found elsewhere. These can come from the Internet or from CDs.

Video clips

Video can be added either from within the program itself or from clips found elsewhere. These can come from the Internet or from TV/video.

Capture audio

The user can record their own sound clips to add to presentations. Most computers come with built in software to do this and all that is needed is a microphone.

Capture Image

The user can add their own pictures taken from a digital camera or scanned in. These could include video images too.

Hyperlinks

These can be placed within a presentation to launch live (or archived) web-pages during the delivery.

Questions

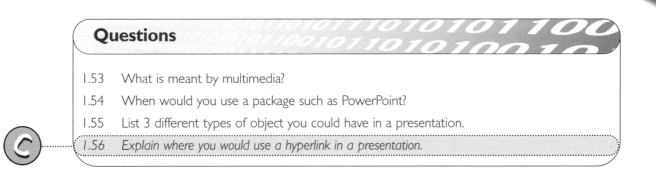

1.53   What is meant by multimedia?

1.54   When would you use a package such as PowerPoint?

1.55   List 3 different types of object you could have in a presentation.

1.56   *Explain where you would use a hyperlink in a presentation.*

WEB PAGE CREATION

Web pages may be created by the user in a number of ways. They can type in all the text and control data in HTML but this is difficult. There are however many packages available to make the task easier by using wizards – programs which step the user through the process - or templates - outlines of commonly used page styles.

Web pages can be made up of several components or elements, including text, graphics, audio (sound files) and video. Usually all of these can be downloaded from the Internet onto the users own computer desktop. Obviously the speed at which these appear on a user's machine is related to their Internet connection speed. A dial-up link will be very slow to download video since the files are large.

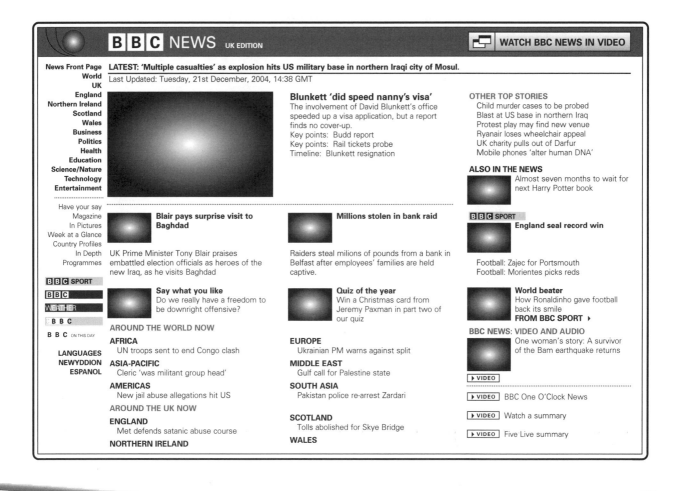

Tables, hotspots and hyperlinks

Web pages can contain additional features to those above such as Tables, where data or pictures are laid out in rows and columns, hotspots, which change as the mouse hovers over them (these can be used for adverts or to give more information on what is beneath the mouse) and hyperlinks which are usually blue in colour with a line under them. These hyperlinks are clickable and take the user to a different web page, or to a different place on the current page, when clicked.

Questions

1.57   Give 2 different ways in a which a web page could be created.

1.58   Give 3 examples of different elements/components on a web page.

1.59   What is meant by

a) hotspot?

b) hyperlink?

INTEGRATION

Some tasks involve using features from more than one package. This can be accomplished in two main ways – multi-task packages and integrated software.

Multi-task packages

A package may be able to do more than one task. For example:

- many spreadsheets allow charts to be created from the spreadsheet data.
- most word-processing packages now have a limited drawing facility.
- data from a database can be merged into standard letters to personalise them.

Static and dynamic links

A static link is broken once the data is transferred from one type of package to another. For example, a drawing is transferred from a drawing package to a word processor. No changes will occur in the copy if the original is then altered.

Tip
most years there is a question in the exam on static and dynamic links

A dynamic link remains live once the data is transferred from one type of package to another. For example, changes to a spreadsheet will immediately be seen in a chart produced from that spreadsheet.

Integrated software / Integrated package

Integrated packages are designed to make the transfer of data from one program to another as simple as possible.

The programs usually share a common Human Computer Interface (HCI) so that they are all operated in a similar way. Many of the pull-down menus are the same as are many of the key combinations for common tasks, such as printing. It is a simple job to combine the features of several programs when producing documents.

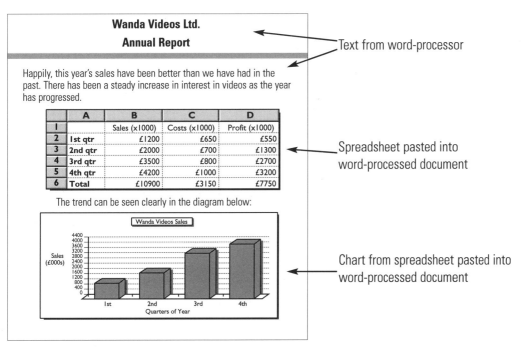

Text from word-processor

Spreadsheet pasted into word-processed document

Chart from spreadsheet pasted into word-processed document

Integration between different packages in a software suite

More sophisticated packages can be sold as a **suite**, meaning they are designed to link together in a way that data can be easily transferred from one element to another. For example, Microsoft Office uses **Excel** and **Word** but data is easily interchanged between these.

With the wide variety of options now available, the user must choose the most appropriate software package or suite based on the hardware available and the task required.

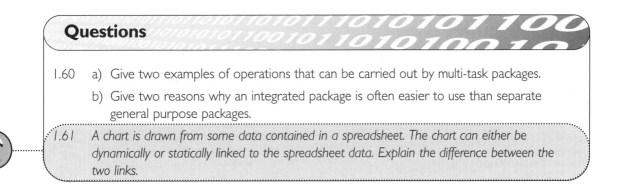

Questions

1.60 a) Give two examples of operations that can be carried out by multi-task packages.

b) Give two reasons why an integrated package is often easier to use than separate general purpose packages.

1.61 *A chart is drawn from some data contained in a spreadsheet. The chart can either be dynamically or statically linked to the spreadsheet data. Explain the difference between the two links.*

IMPLICATIONS

Social

- Some traditional jobs have now largely disappeared. For example, newspapers no longer use compositors as pages are now laid out electronically using Desktop Publishing (DTP) software.

- Some jobs have changed. For example, typists have become word processor operators.

- Many people have retrained for new jobs. Working conditions have improved. For example, there are no longer typing pools and the noise associated with them. However, personal contact and friendship opportunities have also been lost since one word processor operator may now do the work of several typists.

- The number of documents produced has increased since it is now relatively easy for anyone to produce high quality documents using DTP packages.

- It is very easy to produce envelopes or labels with names and addresses taken from a database. These are used to send out the same material to a large number of people by post. This is a mail shot.

Security and privacy

- People now have the right to see what is stored on computer about them. For example, you can ask your bank for a copy of what their computer contains about you. Data stored on computer must be amended if it is found to be incorrect.

- Some groups do not have to say what is on their computers since it may concern crimes or national security. For example, you do not have access rights to the police computers.

- Problems can arise if computer information is out of date or contains mistakes. For example, if a person living near to you had a similar name, he or she might be mistaken for you if the wrong address was entered. To minimise the chances of this, great care must be taken when entering data. For example, double entry checks may be used.

- Since companies now depend greatly on computer data, precautions have to be taken against the data being lost, stolen or altered by unauthorised individuals. Common methods of protection are:
  - keeping computer rooms locked
  - having password access to important files
  - keeping backup copies of vital information in fire- and bomb-proof safes
  - sending data down phone lines as code (encryption) so that computer 'hackers' cannot access it. (A 'hacker' is someone who attempts to gain unauthorised access to a computer system.)

Fears about the increase in the amount of computer data being held led to the Government passing a law in 1984 to guarantee the rights of the individual.

The Data Protection Act 1984 and 1998

- *Any company wishing to hold data on computer about more than a few people must register with a central agency.*

- *Data must be held only for lawful purposes.*

- *Individuals have the right to check what data is held about them by almost any group. Exceptions to this are the police and state security authorities.*

- *Data which is held must be up to date and accurate. If it is not, and this is pointed out, it must be either deleted or amended according to the individuals' wishes.*

- *Data must not be held for longer than is necessary.*

The Computer Misuse Act 1990 makes 'hacking' and malicious acts, such as virus release, illegal. Hacking is the act of trying to gain unauthorised entry to a database or viewdata system. Hacking can be done via the telephone system. This makes hackers very difficult to catch, since they can be many miles away from the computer they access.

The Copyright, Designs and Patents Act 1988 gives the creators of musical, dramatic, literary and artistic work the right to control the ways in which their material may be used. It also includes computer packages. This ensures copies must be bought and not simply passed on from one person to another.

Data user and data subject

A data user is a person who holds and uses personal data about others or controls the use of it.

A data subject is a person about whom personal data is stored by one or more data users.

Setting up costs

The initial costs of setting up a computer system may be very high. These costs include:

Hardware

Hardware consists of all the different components. A computer system can cost from £500 to £4000 each, and a laser printer from £200 to £2000 each.

Software

Application packages can cost from £30 to £1000 or more and integrated packages from £50 to £500.

Training

Computer training costs typically from £200 per day upwards.

Running costs

Running costs include spares, repairs and consumables (for example, discs, paper and toner cartridges).

Hardware has a limited lifespan. It may need to be replaced because it becomes old technology or simply because it wears out.

Staff costs include:

- paying operators and other staff
- paying more to supervisory staff
- paying redundancy money to staff who are no longer required
- paying for training

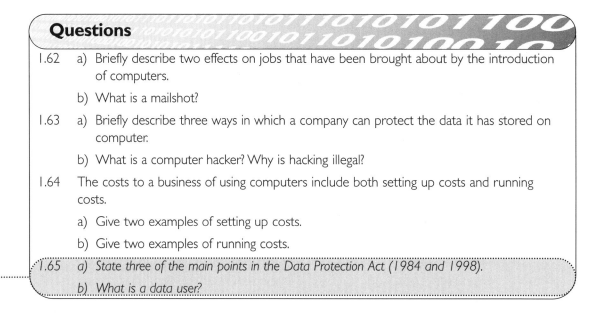

Questions

1.62 a) Briefly describe two effects on jobs that have been brought about by the introduction of computers.

b) What is a mailshot?

1.63 a) Briefly describe three ways in which a company can protect the data it has stored on computer.

b) What is a computer hacker? Why is hacking illegal?

1.64 The costs to a business of using computers include both setting up costs and running costs.

a) Give two examples of setting up costs.

b) Give two examples of running costs.

1.65 a) State three of the main points in the Data Protection Act (1984 and 1998).

b) What is a data user?

Industrial and Commercial Applications

AUTOMATED SYSTEMS

Reasons for automating

Speed

Automated tasks are carried out more quickly. More items can, therefore, be manufactured each day. Repairs can also be carried out more quickly.

Hazardous environment

Machines can do jobs in places where it is unsafe for humans to go – because of extreme temperatures, poisonous fumes, radioactivity or the possibility of explosions.

Repetitive tasks

Humans get bored when carrying out the same task time after time and are more likely to make mistakes. Machines do not get bored and so can do the same thing repeatedly without problems. Each item will be as good as every other one that is produced.

Accuracy

Automated systems can produce exactly the same item in a factory time after time. The accuracy of manufacture is very high.

Efficiency

Above all other reasons, it is economical for manufacturers to automate. The goods produced are less expensive than using traditional manual labour and so the company is more efficient.

Adaptability

Machines can be reprogrammed to do different tasks. They can have different tools attached very quickly. This allows them to be adapted for different uses.

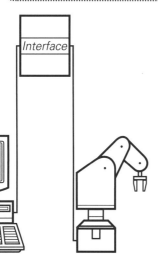

Hardware for automated systems

Input and output devices are connected to the processor.
Input comes from sensors that give information about the surroundings.
Output goes to control motors and machines.

Interfaces

The input and output devices have to communicate with the processor. An interface is used to allow for the differences in speed of operation and codes used by these different devices. The operation of the processor is not delayed by waiting for information to be input or for an output operation to be completed. The interface may be built into the computer system or it may be a part of the device; it may also be a separate box between the two.

Interface

Analogue input and output

- Devices connected to computer systems can provide one of two types of signal.
- Analogue devices give a wide range of signal levels and the value can be any of these levels.
- Analogue signal - continuously variable levels

- Digital devices use binary signals and so have only two levels of signal. These are either high or low and are represented in binary by a 1 or a 0.
- Digital signal – only two levels

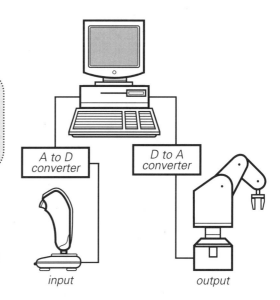

input   output

Converters

The correct interface is required if a computer is to use analogue signals. This is either an Analogue–to-Digital (A-to-D) converter for input, or a Digital-to-Analogue (D-to-A) converter for output.

Input sensors

Humans find out about their surroundings by using their senses – sight, hearing, touch, taste and smell. Machines use sensors in the same way to detect events happening. Typical sensors detect heat, light and movement.

Output devices

A common output device on a computer-controlled machine is a motor. Other devices which are used include lamps and heaters.

Feedback

A computer sends signals to output devices. The computer does not know if its commands have been carried out if no information comes back from the output devices. Information can be sent back to the computer if sensors are fitted to the output device. The **return of information** from the sensors to the computer is described as feedback.

What is a robot?

A robot is a machine which is controlled by computer. However, so is a washing machine but we do not call that a robot! The difference is that the robot is flexible. It can be made to do more than one thing simply by changing the instructions it has been given. The set of instructions is the program for the machine. The robot can carry out many different tasks if it is reprogrammed. A washing machine can only wash things.

The shape of a robot

Many people think that robots have to look like humans. In fact this is usually not the best shape. Reasons why the human shape is not suitable for robots include the following:

- The shape is top heavy and might overbalance.
- It is difficult to make them walk like humans.
- The shape and size might be unsuitable for the work to be done.
- If only one arm is needed then it is wasteful to provide two.

Robot arms

Many robots are only straightforward arms, made with wheels rather than legs if movement is a requirement. These robots operate under the control of a program which can be altered to make them carry out different tasks.

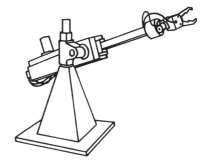

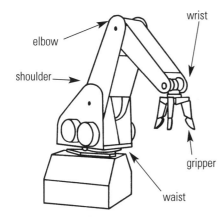

Robot anatomy

A robot arm has a number of joints. The movement of each joint is controlled by computer. Each joint is named in the same way as the joints of a human body. Here is the anatomy of a robot arm:

Tools

Most of the robot arms you see have a simple gripper fitted. There are, however, many other types of tool that can replace this. The tool most suitable for any particular job is fitted. Some arms can change the tool automatically and so carry out a number of different jobs.

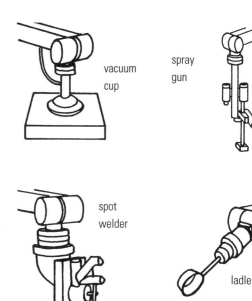

vacuum cup

spray gun

spot welder

ladle

Intelligent robots

*Intelligent robots are advanced robots which can make their own decisions, learn from their mistakes and **adapt** to new experiences. They may be used for military, law enforcement, industry and education.*

Embedded System

An embedded system is a specialized computer system dedicated to a specific task and usually not independently programmable by the user. Embedded systems are often used in medical and manufacturing equipment.

Stationary and mobile robots

Many robots are simply arms fixed in position on the floor of a factory. These are called stationary robots.

There are some situations where a robot is required to move from one place to another. In this case mobile robots are used. They usually move using wheels or tracks driven by motors.

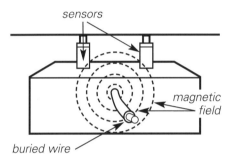

Magnetic guides

Some mobile robots are able to follow a track that is formed by a wire buried in the ground. An electric current is passed through the wire and this generates a magnetic field. Sensors on the robot can detect this and follow the path of the wire.

Light guides

Some mobile robots are able to follow a white line on the floor. They do this by shining a light onto the floor and detecting the reflected light with two light sensors. If the robot is centred over the line, then both sensors give an equal signal. If the robot is not over the line, then unequal signals are detected. The control program will make the robot move back over the line again.

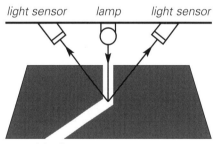

CAD/CAM

CAD/CAM stands for Computer Aided Design/Computer Aided Manufacture.

CAD uses computers in design processes. Once something has been designed using the computer, it can be viewed from all angles on the screen. Changes can easily be made and the final design details can be sent on to the manufacturing process. CAM uses machines controlled by the computer to manufacture things. This has all the advantages of using automated systems.

Programming robots

A program can be written which tells the robot exactly what has to be done. However, this is not the best way for some processes, especially when the programmer is trying to copy operations normally done by humans. It is sometimes better in these cases to use a lead-through method, where the movements of a human operator using a tool are recorded by a computer. The computer then uses this information to control a robot to carry out the same actions.

Programming languages

The instructions given to the machine will usually be written using a high-level programming language. This makes it easy for the programmer to change the instructions and correct any errors in the program. Each instruction will often correspond to a movement or set of movements of the machine. For example, one instruction might tell it to move through a given distance or to bend by a given angle.

Control languages

The operator needs to give instructions to an automated device which are specific to the needs of machines controlled by computers. Special control languages have been developed to do this.

The software for controlling a particular device can be very specific and may be stored in customised ROM.

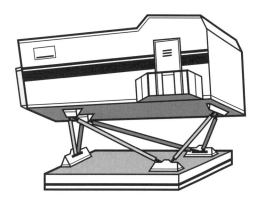

Simulation

Some real-life activities can be highly dangerous or very expensive to carry out. Situations ranging from defusing bombs or controlling nuclear power stations, to flying aeroplanes or driving large trucks, can be realistically simulated using automated systems. Simulation allows the process to be studied safely and at reasonable cost.

Simulators are computer-controlled and may use hydraulic systems to produce realistic movements. Visual effects are presented on screens.

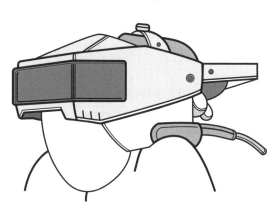

Virtual reality (VR) is a form of simulation where the movements of the user are translated into screen changes by the computer. VR can use gloves and headsets so the user experiences the actual environment of the simulation and the computer responds to their movements.

Real-time operation

Real-time operation uses the computer to process events as they happen. The output from the computer depends on the input it receives – different input data will cause different instructions to be given out. For example, an automated factory must respond at once when anything happens, such as a piece of machinery breaking down or when running low on parts for a process. To do this, it works in real-time.

Retraining

People have learnt how to use automated systems as they have been introduced. This has often meant going on retraining courses to help them understand the new technology. Employees are often worried about this since they feel they might not be able to understand the new machines. Usually their fears have been unfounded as most have managed to cope well with the new equipment. Many find their jobs more satisfying once the robot or other machine has taken over the boring jobs.

Employment

Employees have seen their jobs change with the introduction of automation. Their working conditions have improved and there is a general increase in leisure time. Britain also produces robots for export and this has helped to increase the number of jobs.

Safety

All machines can be dangerous to humans. Those running under computer control are no exception, and so they have many safety features built into them. For example, they may not operate if anyone is in a dangerous position. Safety gates and sensors enable the systems to operate with the least chance of injuring anyone.

Costs

It costs a lot to build a factory or warehouse that uses automated systems. However, once these are built and equipped, they are very much less expensive to run than traditional factories. Fewer workers are required. Areas that contain only machines do not need to be so warm or well lit as areas where humans work. The long term savings are large. The only costs are those of maintaining the equipment and replacing it when it wears out or becomes obsolete.

Financial implications

Traditional factories are both capital and labour intensive. They cost a lot of money to set up and keep running. All facilities have to be provided for the employees. The workforce has to be paid and this can be very expensive. Automated factories can be designed to be much cheaper to build and run and so provide a better investment. Productivity in automated factories can be much higher than that in traditional ones, although the initial cost of machinery is high.

Design considerations

Places where automated systems work are different to those where humans work. They are carefully designed after an analysis of the exact requirements of the systems to be used has been made. This is called a systems analysis and looks at the whole production process and which parts can be computerised. More and more factories are being automated.

Questions

2.1 a) Briefly describe four benefits to companies which use automated systems.

   b) Explain why an interface is used with automated systems.

2.2 Two types of signal are used when devices are connected to computer systems: analogue and digital. Draw diagrams to show these signals and explain the difference between them.

2.3 a) What is a sensor and what type of device is it?

   b) Name three types of sensor.

2.4 Name three types of output device used with automated systems.

2.5 a) What is feedback?

   b) What kind of device is attached to output devices to allow feedback to take place?

2.6. *Explain what is meant when automated computer systems are said to be adaptable.*

2.7   *A-to-D and D-to-A converters are special types of interface. Explain what they are and which is used for input and which for output.*

2.8   a) Give a brief explanation of what a robot is.

        b) Give three reasons why a robot is usually not shaped like a human.

2.9   Draw a diagram of a robot arm to show the following joints:

        shoulder; elbow; gripper; waist; wrist.

2.10   a) What name is used to describe a robot that is fixed in position?

        b) What do mobile robots usually use to move about?

2.11   a) A magnetic guide can be used to guide a mobile robot around a factory. Briefly describe how this system works.

        b) Name one other guidance system for mobile robots.

2.12   Expand and briefly describe the abbreviations CAD/CAM.

2.13   Briefly describe two methods of programming robots.

2.14   a) Which of the following types of language is best for a programmer to use to program a computer that is controlling a robot:

        high-level, assembly, low-level or machine code?

        b) Explain why you have made this choice.

2.15   a) Give three examples of situations which are suitable for computer simulation. In each case give one reason why this is suitable.

        b) Describe how movement and visual effects are typically produced by simulators.

2.16   a) What is meant when a process is said to take place in real-time?

        b) Give an example of a real-time process.

2.17   a) Give one example of worries employees might have when automated systems are introduced into a factory.

        b) Give two examples of benefits to employees from the introduction of automated systems.

        c) Explain why the running costs of factories using automated systems are much lower than those which are not automated.

2.18   *a) Explain why special control languages were developed for programming automated systems.*

        b) Other than in backing store, where might the specialised programs be stored?

COMMERCIAL DATA PROCESSING

Volume of documents

Large organisations need to process a great amount of data every day. These include banks, mail order companies, high street stores, supermarkets, those who manufacture and distribute goods, and service industries such as gas, electricity and telephone companies.

Speed of processing

Computers are ideal for accurate processing of data at high speed. It would take much longer for this to be done by humans alone.

Repetitive tasks

When humans do the same task continuously, they get tired and may make mistakes. Computers can work for 24 hours a day doing the same task accurately.

Speed of access

The data that is stored by computers can be rapidly found, even on terminals far from the main computer. This access would be very much slower if the same data was stored on paper.

Management information

Computers which process data produce information. Managers use this information to help them run their organisations efficiently. This information is often presented as graphs and charts to make it easy to understand.

The Data Processing cycle

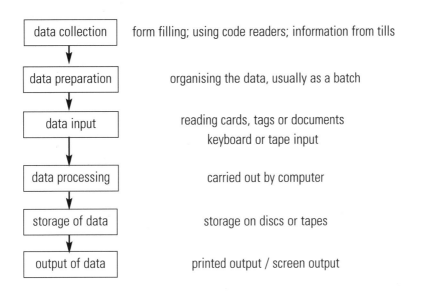

data collection	form filling; using code readers; information from tills
data preparation	organising the data, usually as a batch
data input	reading cards, tags or documents keyboard or tape input
data processing	carried out by computer
storage of data	storage on discs or tapes
output of data	printed output / screen output

Data and information

The terms **data** and **information** are often used to mean the same thing. However, strictly speaking, data is any information that can be stored in a computer and is meaningless without other facts. Information is data in a form that means something to humans – it is data put into context.

For example, the data item 12345 stored in a computer could refer to almost anything. It could be a number for arithmetic, a telephone number, the code number of a stock item in a store, the earnings of someone for a year – or many other things. It becomes information as soon as it is made meaningful to us by the statement:

Cost of new car = £12 345

Collection and input of data

A number of different methods are used to simplify the collection and entry of data. They are all intended to eliminate operator errors which can happen when figures have to be entered manually. A suitable reader for each method is used for data input.

Bar codes

Bar codes are found on groceries, books, periodicals, stationery and consumer goods.

Magnetic stripes

Magnetic stripes are used on cheque and credit cards to allow the card details to be entered automatically.

Magnetic ink character recognition (MICR)

Magnetic ink characters are used on cheques for the automatic reading of account details.

Mark sense cards

Marks are made on cards which can be read by special card-reading equipment. This method is used, for example, for stock control and recording examination answers.

Optical Character recognition (OCR)

Optical character readers are very sensitive to the font and size of characters that they can read. There are uses in business (to save retyping documents on paper) and in stock control (for example, reading till rolls).

Other input methods

Smart Cards

These are cards about the size of a credit card that contain a computer chip which can hold and process information. They can store personal information, hold digital cash or prove identity.

A check digit is often added to numerical data to check that the data has been correctly entered into the computer. The check digit is calculated from the other numbers in the data and added to the end of the data. The computer recalculates the check digit when the number is entered and compares the result of this calculation to the check digit at the end of the number. If they are different, the data has been entered incorrectly and so is discarded and has to be entered again. For example, International Standard Book Numbers (ISBNs, used to identify books), credit card numbers and bank card numbers use check digits.

The check digit can be the character X as well as the numbers 0 to 9 in some types of calculation. For example, the Notes for Standard Grade Physics in this revision series have the ISBN 1–898890–76–5

Other types of checks

Range checks

A range check can be made on data to see if it is in the expected range. For example, if data is input which refers to pupils in secondary school, the age range is usually from 11 to 18 years old. Any age outside this is suspect and could well be an error. A range check will allow the program to ask for suspect numbers to be checked by the user.

Length check

A simple check on data is to check its length. It may be incorrect if it is longer than expected. For example, a stock reference may contain up to six characters. If the data that is input contains more than six characters, then it must be wrong. This can be helped, by careful design of forms when the information is entered manually. Six spaces for the numbers indicate how many digits are required.

Reliability of checks

While many kinds of check can be made on data that is input, there is no guarantee that the data is always 100% correct. There is a possibility that the data entered is wrong and this must be recognised by users.

Validation of data

Data which is valid is within prescribed limits. A range check can be made on data that is input to make sure that it is valid. For example, a day of the month must be between 1 and 31. The computer can check to see if data input is within these limits (and, more accurately, take the number of days in each month into account) i.e. does the data makes sense.

Verification of data

Data which is input to computers must be accurate. Mechanical input is more reliable than human input. Data typed in at a keyboard is more likely to contain errors than that input using a bar code reader.

One way to reduce human error is to use double entry. Two different operators enter the data. The computer compares both sets and if there are any differences both sets are deleted and have to be input again. Alternatively a user can be asked a YES/NO question to verify data with that stored on file.

Storing data

Data is stored in files. Each file contains a record for each item or transaction. Each record contains a number of fields. This is the same structure as a database.

Updating data

As the data is processed, new information has to be stored. Updating means adding the new data to that which is already stored.

Backup

Companies could be put out of business if they lost their data. To prevent this happening, a second copy is made every time the data is updated. This backup copy can be used if the main file is damaged or accidentally or deliberately lost.

Processing data

Interactive processing

The program runs continuously and reacts to what is input. The result of processing this input decides what the next action is to be. This type of processing is used where an immediate result is required. Examples include operating bank accounts, control of machinery, applications such as word-processing and booking holidays or theatre seats. This is also described as real-time processing.

File access methods

Sequential access

Sequential (serial) access is used to store data on tape systems. The data is stored one item after another. To access the data, each item has to be read in the order in which it was stored. To get to a given item, all previous items have to be read – this is time-consuming. Sequential access is most suitable when large amounts of data have to be read or written only occasionally. It is mainly used for backup purposes and for keeping master files. It can also be used to make up a transaction file when the data is added as each item comes in.

Random (direct) access

The data is written to the storage wherever the system decides. There is no prescribed order. Similarly, the data can be read in any order by going directly to the point where it is stored. This is typical of disc storage systems and is used where constant changes are being made to the data and in interactive systems.

Multi-user database

This is a database either on a network or on the Internet that can have two or more users at the same time, appearing to each as if they are the sole user.

Hardware for CDP

A mainframe computer may be needed to cope with the quantity of data being used in Commercial Data Processing. It has to be fast and able to address a large amount of memory. Attached to this computer are many terminals which are simply screens with keyboards. All the processing is done by the mainframe. There will be several high speed printers for hard copy output. The backing storage devices need to be both magnetic tape (for transaction files and backup files) and magnetic disc (for storing data for interactive processing).

Output methods

Output to screen

Screen output is used to allow the computer to communicate with the operator.

Output to paper

Hard copy is used for printed output for staff and customers. This is often done on high speed printers.

Output to file

Output can also be sent to file ready for processing later. This may be a print spool file or a temporary, partially processed file.

Jobs and careers

- The **Programmer** writes the programs used to process the data and also modifies existing programs to meet new demands.
- The **Systems Analyst** decides on the software and hardware required for a particular application.
- The **Engineer** maintains the computer systems and repairs them if they break down.
- The **Network Manager** has overall responsibility to maintain a Local Area Network usually within one company.

The costs of Commercial Data Processing

Initial costs: the cost of the computers, printers, backing storage and consumables is only part of the initial cost of setting up a data processing department. Software costs can be as high as hardware costs. There is also the cost of buying the furniture, telephones and the building to house everything.

Running costs include the salaries of staff, training, electricity and consumables (for example, paper, discs, ink). Repairs and spare parts for the computers and renting buildings are other running costs.

E-Commerce

Any exchange of goods or services via the Internet is known as e-commerce. Many firms now have web sites which often sell more than their traditional shops. Firms such as Amazon.com® have shown that companies which operate only online can be successful. So-called online shopping has seen a huge increase in recent years as users become more confident about web security.

Online banking

Most High street banks now offer an online service too. This allows customers to log in to a secure website with their own ID and password and then access their bank accounts to pay bills, move money etc.

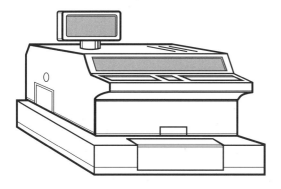

Point of Sale Terminals (POST)

The terminals are programmed with the costs of all the items in the shop. A reader (usually for bar codes) is used to enter the sale details. There is little chance of assistants making mistakes in entering prices or of price labels falling off or being exchanged. The prices must be kept up-to-date as they change.

Electronic Funds Transfer (EFT)

No money is handed over when a customer buys something using EFT. The funds are instead transferred almost immediately from the customer's bank account to that of the business. This is done using a computer linking the business to the bank's computer.

Computer crime

It is estimated that many millions of pounds are lost every year because of computer fraud when people steal money electronically. Another example of computer crime is theft of information. This may be for many purposes – for example, to find out about a competitor's prices in order to tender a lower bid, or to steal valuable information about the manufacture of goods. A further example is the deliberate destruction or corruption of a competitor's data to put them out of business.

Accuracy

Accuracy of information is very important. The details of goods in store and of sales allow enough stock to be available without over-stocking. Customer details are equally important, because the company needs to know for example who owes it money. This, and other stored information, must be accurate for the company to run efficiently.

Current legislation

The Data Protection Act covers the customer details stored by companies. Under this Act the customer has the right to:

- *expect these details to be accurate and used properly*
- *see the details stored about them by the company*
- *instruct the company not to pass his or her details on to other companies. You will often see an indication on forms which you fill in that allows you to take this option. Many people are concerned about the amount of 'junk mail' that they receive. This happens in many cases because customer details are passed from one company to another.*

The Computer Misuse Act 1990 prohibits unofficial users from accessing the computers either locally (from the building) or remotely (by telephone from another town).

The Copyright, Designs and Patents Act 1988 makes it illegal to make unauthorised copies of downloaded material, like music or video files.

Privacy

A company does not want its competitors to find out details about its business. Equally, customers expect the details of their transactions with a company to be kept confidential. A company must make sure that only authorised persons gain access to the data stored in its computers.

Security

Organisations take security measures to prevent unauthorised access to their computer files. Different passwords give access to different levels of information in the computer. The password does not appear on the screen when it is typed in. A data preparation operator will enter a password that gives access only to the data entry programs. A manager will need access to much more detailed information and so will enter a different password to gain access to more of the files. Access to the computer areas will also be restricted to those people who work there. They may need to use cards or special codes to gain access to the computer buildings.

Sale of customer lists

Some companies have large lists of their customers which are of interest to other organisations. They may be willing to sell these. The buyer may ask for lists of people who live in a certain part of the country, who are in a certain range of age or income or who have particular jobs or interests.

The manual system

In the past, all companies used manual systems for data processing. Large books (ledgers) were used to detail everything that happened and much paper was stored in filing cabinets. Many office staff were required to prepare and keep the records in order.

All this can now be done by fewer people using a computerised system. Finding information is much faster this way and much less paper has to be stored. The company runs more efficiently and their costs are lower as a result. Some companies still run both systems together in case there are problems.

Single entry, multiple use

It is inefficient if the operator has to enter similar information more than once. A typical example of this is the name and address of a customer. This has to be entered when the customer first starts using a company. Later, when first payments are made, perhaps the address is entered again. This is unnecessary if the customer details are already stored in the files. By allocating some unique identifier (such as a customer number) there is no need for multiple entries (and storage) of similar information. The organisation of data storage also helps. The software needs to support single entry of data for multiple purposes (e.g. relational databases).

The size of businesses

It is important to appreciate the scale of big businesses. The number of customers may be tens or even hundreds of thousands. Each day thousands or tens of thousands of transactions take place. A large company will employ hundreds or even thousands of staff, both to process the transactions and in the manufacture, storage and distribution of its products.

Questions

2.19 a) Briefly describe three reasons why companies use computers to process their data.

     b) List the main stages in the data processing cycle.

2.20 a) Explain the difference between data and information.

     b) Give an example to support your answer.

2.21 a) Name three methods of collection and input of data to a computer which are designed to eliminate operator errors.

     b) Suggest one use for each method you have selected.

2.22 a) What is a check digit?

     b) Give two examples of situations where check digits are used.

     c) What characters are usually used as check digits?

     d) Name two other types of check that are often made on the data which has been entered into a computer.

2.23 a) *Describe the process of Optical Character Recognition.*

     b) *What textual features are important when using optical character readers?*

     c) *Name two uses of Optical Character Recognition.*

2.24 a) Explain what is meant by the term interactive processing.

     b) Give an example of where it would be used.

2.25 a) *Explain the term validation of data.*

     b) *Describe the process of double entry of data.*

     c) *Is double entry an example of validation or verification?*

2.26 a) *What type of media is typically used for storing data by sequential access?*

     b) *What type of media is typically used for storing data by direct access?*

     c) *Give an alternative name for each of the above storage methods.*

     d) *Name a typical use of sequential access files.*

2.27 Briefly describe the main hardware required by a large company which processes its data by computer.

2.28 a) Briefly describe the work done by each of the following employees:

        programmer; engineer; network manager

     b) Name one other job associated with commercial data processing.

2.29 a) Name some of the initial costs involved when a company decides to use commercial data processing.

     b) Name some of the running costs involved when a company uses commercial data processing.

2.30 a) What is a point-of-sale terminal?

     b) What advantage to the company exists when point-of-sale terminals are used?

     c) Explain the process of electronic funds transfer.

2.31   a) *Commercial data processed output can be to file. What happens to the file at a later stage?*

      b) *Name two different types of file that may be used.*

2.32   *Briefly describe two examples of computer crime.*

2.33   Security is very important to commercial organisations. One method of keeping files secure is to allow access by the use of passwords.

      a) Describe what happens on such a system when a user wants to access the information.

      b) Why might there be more than one password in use?

      c) Describe one other method of maintaining security of data.

2.34   Some commercial companies will sell lists of their customers to other companies. What advantage is there for the company buying the lists?

2.35   Briefly compare the manual system by which companies maintain their records with a modern computerised system.

Systems: Software and hardware

SYSTEMS SOFTWARE

Software

The instructions given to a computer system telling it what to do are called software. A complete set of instructions is called a **program**.

Low-level languages

Computers use binary code (patterns of 0 and 1) to represent instructions and data. This is low-level language.

It is difficult for humans to understand this machine code and to trace and correct errors in it.

For example, a machine code instruction to print the letter B may be:

10101001 01000010 00010100 11101110 11111111

High-level languages

High-level languages use English words to give instructions to a computer. High-level languages are needed because humans find them easier to understand and therefore programming is made simpler.

For example, a high-level language instruction to print the letter B may be:

PRINT 'B'

Common features

High-level languages use specific words which are put together to make up a program instructing the computer what to do. One high-level language instruction represents several machine code instructions. The instructions are carried out in sequence, one after another. Most high-level languages have commands for process, repetition and decisions.

For example: process –   PRINT   repetition –   FOR ... NEXT
                 decisions –   IF ... THEN

Translation

The process of changing the commands in a high-level language to machine code is called **translation**. It is necessary since a computer processor cannot understand a high-level language so any programs written must be translated into machine code.

Portable software can be run on a number of different computer systems. Ideally, no changes are required to the software to let it run on different machines. In practice, minor changes are often required to allow the software to run.

Types of translator – Compiler

The program is written using a text editor or word processor. This is the **source code**. The compiler converts the whole of the source code to machine code. This is the **object code**. This object code is loaded into the computer's memory and executed. It will operate far more quickly than a similar interpreted program because it does not have to be translated further. However, any errors in the program (either as the program is being compiled or when the program is being executed) cannot be corrected on the object code. The programmer must go back to the source code, correct the errors and compile it again before it can be executed.

Types of translator – Interpreter

The program is usually written using the text editor built into the language. This high-level code is translated one line at a time into machine code which is immediately executed. Interpreted languages operate much more slowly than compiled languages. This is because each line has to be translated before it can be executed. This is time-consuming. Loops run slowly because every line in the loop has to be translated every time it operates. Interpreted languages are easier to correct because changes can be made to the program immediately.

Compiled or Interpreted languages

A high-level language is usually either a compiled language or an interpreted language. Some, however, can be both. For example, PASCAL is usually a compiled language but interpreted versions do exist. BASIC is usually an interpreted language. However, versions of BASIC exist which use a compiler rather than an interpreter and so run much more quickly on any particular system.

Summary

The choice of which type of translator to use depends on the type of program being written and the experience of the program writer. Complex programs written by experienced programmers for system software or applications tend to use compilers or assemblers.

Translator	Speed	Easy to alter	Easy to understand
Interpreter	slow	yes	yes
Compiler	fast	no	yes

Questions

3.1   a) Describe the main features of high-level languages.

      b) What name is given to the process of turning a high-level language program into machine code?

3.2   a) Explain the difference between source code and object code when using a compiler.

      b) Explain what a programmer must do when making changes to a compiled program.

      c) Explain why interpreted programs run more slowly than compiled programs.

OPERATING AND FILING SYSTEMS

The operating system

An operating system is a set of programs that give instructions to the computer which tell it what to do. The operating system takes charge when the computer is switched on. All the processes that happen in the computer are under the operating system's control, including housekeeping programs and providing the HCI for the user.

Functions of an operating system

Memory management controls where programs are located in memory, where data is put in memory and what the system has to remember.

File management organises the data that is sent to files on backing storage and controls the loading of files into memory.

Input/output controls reading the keyboard and other input devices. It controls the sending of data to output devices such as the VDU and printer.

Job scheduler organises the way in which different tasks are carried out and gives control of the CPU to faster processes wherever possible.

Error reporting informs the user if any problems occur.

Types of operating system

A **batch** operating system is set up to carry out batch processing (i.e. many items at one time). Similarly, an **interactive** operating system is set up to carry out interactive processing (see page 60).

Operating systems as a human computer interface

The operating system provides a human computer interface in that it allows the user and the computer to communicate with each other by mouse, keyboard and screen.

Background jobs

Interactive operating systems can spend a large amount of processor time waiting for something to happen. Other tasks can be carried out in this idle time. These are called background tasks and are suspended as soon as the main task requires the processor. For example, most time in a word processor is spent waiting for characters to be typed in at the keyboard. The processor operates very much more quickly than the human typing in characters at the keyboard – it probably spends less than 1% of its time working. There is plenty of time to do other things. Background printing can, for example, be carried out. Instead of the processor being fully committed to the job of sending data to a printer (this is a very slow process compared to the speed of operation of the processor), the data to be printed is spooled (saved) to disc. Whenever the processor is not committed to any other task, it can send some more of this data to the printer. Although the printer may sometimes have to wait because the processor is busy, the main application can therefore continue in real-time and the printing goes on as a background task.

Directories or catalogues

These two words have the same meaning. Part of the operating system is responsible for the information stored on backing storage (the file manager). It has to maintain the information about the files stored on the disc or tape - how many there are, where they are and how large they are. Each time new information is written, the directory or catalogue must be updated. This happens every time a new file is added, a file is deleted or a file is modified. In the case of discs, a part of the disc is used to store this information. The operating system looks at this part first before reading or writing files. In a modern computer system the directory is shown graphically as a **folder**.

Types of file

Two main types of file are stored:

Data files contain the data to be operated on by programs or applications. An example is the text produced by a word-processing program.

Program files contain the instructions telling the computer what to do to make a particular program or application work. An example is a word-processing program.

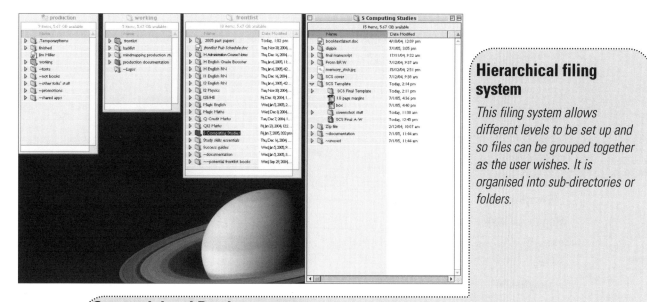

Hierarchical filing system

This filing system allows different levels to be set up and so files can be grouped together as the user wishes. It is organised into sub-directories or folders.

Sequential and Random access

Data can be accessed by a computer in two ways. Sequential or serial access means the data is read from the beginning through to the end. Tapes work this way and so it is more suited to backup. Random or direct access involves discs where one piece can be read or written to directly by simply going to its location on the disc. This is used in interactive or real-time applications.

Questions

3.3   a) What is an operating system?

       b) Name four of the functions of an operating system.

       c) What advantage is there in storing the operating system in RAM rather than ROM?

3.4   a) What is the difference between data files and program files?

       b) Give an example of each type of file.

       c) What is the purpose of a directory on a disc?

3.5   Interactive operating systems can often carry out background tasks.

       a) Why are these tasks suited to interactive systems?

       b) Give one example of a background task.

LOW-LEVEL MACHINE

Bit

A bit is a Binary Digit, either a 0 or a 1.

Byte

A group of eight bits is called a byte.

Kilobyte(Kb)

A kilobyte is approximately 1 000 bytes. It is actually the nearest power of 2 to 1000. One kilobyte is exactly 1 024 bytes.

Megabyte(Mb)

A megabyte is approximately a million bytes. It is actually the nearest power of 2 to 1000 000. One megabyte is exactly 1 048 576 bytes.

Gigabyte(Gb)

A gigabyte is approximately 1000 Megabytes. It is actually the nearest power of 2 to 1000 000 000. One gigabyte is exactly 1024 Megabytes.

Terabyte(Tb)

A Terabyte is approximately 1000 Gigabytes or one trillion bytes. One Terabyte is exactly 1024 Gigabytes.

Input – Process – Output

Input is data that is passed into the processor to be processed. Output is the result of that processing being passed to output devices.

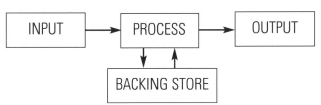

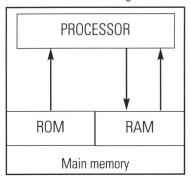

Central Processing Unit

Central Processing Unit (CPU)

The CPU is where the processing takes place in a computer. It contains two main parts, the processor and main memory. Main memory is made of two parts – Read-only memory (ROM) and Random Access Memory (RAM).

Machine code

A computer is a digital device. It works using sets of ones and zeros to represent data and instructions. Machine code is a collection of these numbers that the computer uses for operations, so no further translation is required. Any other type of instructions (low-level language or high-level language) has to be translated into machine code before it can be understood by the computer.

Advantage

The advantage in using machine code is that it is executed very quickly, much faster than a high-level language. This is because the machine code does not have to be translated before it is used by the processor.

Disadvantages

There are a number of problems in using machine code:

- It is difficult for humans to understand because it is just numbers.
- Typing in many numbers can lead to error.
- It is difficult to find and correct these errors.
- Programs are often quite long.
- Programs can be hard to plan since the instructions relate to the way in which machines work.

Words

A word, in computing terms, is a collection of bits treated as a single unit by the processor. In practice, this usually refers to the number of bits moved as a group, either as instructions or as data. This is typically 8 bits, but groups of 16 bits, 32 bits or 64 bits are also used. For example, here is an 8-bit word:

11000101

Addressability

An address is a storage location. The processor uses a number to identify it. This number is unique, so there is only one location with any particular address. The addressability of a particular processor relates to the number of different addresses that it can normally use. Older processors have addressabilities of 64 Kb; more recent ones can address 16 Mb and others address 4096 Mb (4 Gigabytes).

How the computer stores numbers

Numbers in a computer are stored as binary numbers. They use the digits 0 and 1 only. Each binary digit represents a power of two. Starting at the right of a number, the first digit shows how many units the number contains. The next digit to the left shows the number of twos; then fours, eights, sixteens, etc.

This is best shown by a diagram:

place value	8	4	2	1
binary number	1	1	1	0

This represents the decimal number 14. This is calculated as:

1×8 + 1×4 + 1×2 + 0×1 = 14

When there are more binary digits, the one at the right always has the place value one:

place value	128	64	32	16	8	4	2	1
binary number	1	1	1	0	0	1	1	1

This represents the decimal number 231. This is calculated as:

1×128 + 1×64 + 1×32 + 1×4 + 1×2 + 1×1

A binary number with 4 **bits** can represent decimal numbers in the range 0 to 15.

A binary number with 8 **bits** can represent decimal numbers in the range 0 to 255.

How the computer stores text

Text includes all the letters of the alphabet (both capital and small letters), punctuation marks (.,;:? etc.), arithmetic symbols (+-*/ etc.) and numbers (if they are not to be used for calculations). A binary number is used to represent each character. This number is in a code called ASCII (American Standard Code for Information Interchange). ASCII codes are normally in the decimal range 32 to 127.

One byte can be used to store any one character. Here are some ASCII codes and the characters they represent:

code	character
65	A
99	c
50	2
43	+

How the computer stores graphics

One way that the computer represents graphics uses pixels. A pixel is a picture element, the smallest element of a graphic. Each one can be either on or off. This will turn the colour on or off. One bit represents one pixel in a black and white picture.

These pictures use 64 pixels to make up each graphic character.

Resolution of graphics

Resolution is a measure of the number of pixels used to store a picture. Higher resolution means a greater number of pixels, and so more detail.

64 pixels

low resolution

256 pixels

higher resolution

64 pixels

low resolution

256 pixels

higher resolution

Character sets

Each ASCII code represents a different character. The group of characters described by a range of ASCII codes is called a character set. There are different character sets because different countries use different characters. Also, some character sets contain graphic characters rather than letters, numbers, punctuation and mathematical symbols. For example:

Part of one character set: ABCDEF12345!@£$%=+-"vwxyz

Part of another character set: ABXΔE12345!≠≤æ%+=-©√∑≈¥Ω

In the examples above, some characters are the same. The same ASCII code represents the same character. In other parts of the character sets, the same ASCII code represents different characters:

code	character in first set	character in second set
65	A	A
68	D	Δ

Integers

Integers are whole numbers. The computer stores them as binary numbers. The largest integer that a computer can store depends on the number of bits used. For example, if four bits are used, then the smallest binary number is 0000 and the largest is 1111. This gives a decimal range of 0 to 15.

If eight bits are used, the range is from 00000000 to 11111111 binary (0 to 255 decimal). Many computers use 32 bits with a largest possible integer number of 4 294 967 295.

Storing large numbers

Computers can store very large numbers. They have to lose some accuracy to do this. The numbers are stored in floating point format. For example, a decimal number such as 123 456 789 can be shown as the two numbers 0.123456789×10^9. The number 0.123456789 is the mantissa and the number 9 is the exponent.

The numbers stored in the computer are, of course, binary numbers. A binary number stored in floating point form might be:

$1001011010010110 \times 2^{10010110}$

The same system is used to store non-integer (real) numbers.

Processor structure

The processor consists of three main areas:

The Control Unit supervises the execution of program instructions. This involves the flow of data between memory and the processor and operations inside the processor.

The ALU is the Arithmetic and Logic Unit. It performs arithmetical operations, such as addition and subtraction of numbers. It also performs logical operations, for example AND and OR.

*Registers are storage areas within the CPU itself; because of this they are very fast to access. The most common is called the **accumulator**.*

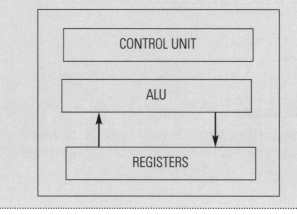

Questions

3.6   Explain the terms bit, byte, kilobyte, megabyte, gigabyte and terabyte.

3.7   a)   Draw a diagram to show the relationship between input, output, process and backing store. Add arrows to show the direction in which data flows.

         b)   Name the two main parts of the Central Processing Unit.

3.8   a)   Explain why the execution of machine code is much faster than the execution of a high-level language.

         b)   Give two reasons why programmers do not program in machine code.

3.9   a)   Explain why the binary number 1110 represents the decimal number 14.

         b)   Give the decimal place values for each of the eight digits in an 8 bit number.

3.10   Textual information in a computer is represented by ASCII codes for each character.

         a)   Expand the term ASCII.

         b)   Give an example of an ASCII code and the character it represents.

         c)   How many bytes are needed to store each character represented by an ASCII code?

3.11   *a)   Explain the term word when used in computing.*

         b)   Explain the term addressability

3.12   a)   What is a pixel?

         b)   Explain how the resolution of graphics depends on the number of pixels used.

3.13   a)   What is a character set?

         b)   What differences might there be between different character sets?

3.14   *Give two examples to describe the function of control characters.*

3.15   *a)   Explain the term integer number.*

         b)   What is the range of integer binary numbers if eight bits are available to store them?

         c)   What is this range as decimal values?

3.16   *Computers store numbers which may not be whole numbers as a mantissa and exponent.*

         a)   Give a name for this storage method.

         b)   Give an example of a binary number stored as a mantissa and exponent. Indicate which part is the mantissa and which the exponent.

3.17   *a)   What is the purpose of the control unit in the Central Processing Unit?*

         b)   Name a typical logic operation carried out in the Arithmetic and Logic Unit.

         c)   In computing terms what is meant by the term register?

3.18   *How much memory would be required to store a black and white display with resolution 800 x 600?*

HARDWARE

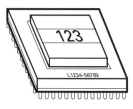

The microprocessor

The microprocessor controls everything that takes place in a microcomputer. It is an example of a silicon chip – many thousands of tiny electronic components manufactured on a thin slice of silicon. It controls other chips in the computer which are used for purposes such as memory, operating systems, languages and to control input and output.

Types of Computer

The main computer types in use today are listed below:

Mainframe

A large powerful computer serving hundreds or even thousands of users, usually kept in a special air-conditioned room is called a mainframe computer.

Desktop

The computer you use at school or at home is probably a desktop. It is a computer small enough to fit into an individual workspace. Modern examples usually come with built in CD drives or DVDs.

Laptop

A laptop is a portable yet powerful computer with a screen that folds away when not in use. Laptops can run off batteries for up to several hours and so may be used anywhere. Also called a notebook.

Palmtop

A palmtop is the smallest type of computer which is handheld. Also known as a PDA (Personal Digital Assistant) or a Pocket PC. Some have small keyboards, some have a stylus for writing. These can be connected to a desktop to share/backup data.

Tablet PC

Low specification laptops with no keyboard are called tablet PCs. A stylus is used for input and they tend to have a long battery life. They look like an A4 pad and can be used standing up – like an electronic-clipboard.

Memory

Memory chips are either ROM or RAM:

ROM (Read Only Memory): The contents of ROM can only be read, not altered. The contents are not lost when the computer is switched off. ROM is used, for example, to store operating systems and languages.

RAM (Random Access Memory): The contents of RAM can be read and altered. The contents are usually lost when the computer is switched off. RAM is used, for example, to store programs and data.

Storage locations

Memory is organised as storage locations. Each unit of memory has its own address (a number) which the processor uses to read from or write to. There is only one location with any particular address.

Backing store

RAM usually loses its contents when the computer is turned off. The contents must be saved to backing store if they are needed again. Magnetic media such as discs or tapes are mainly used. They are easy to remove from one computer and use on a different computer.

Cassette tapes were once commonly used for microcomputers but are no longer used. Mainframe computers use large tape drives to store considerable amounts of data.

Storage capacity

The storage capacity of floppy discs is typically between 80 Kb and 1.44 Mb. Hard discs store larger amounts, typically up to 300 Gb.

Floppy discs contain a thin plastic disc coated with magnetic material. The outer case supports the disc as it spins round and helps keep dirt off the disc surface. Great care must be taken not to touch the disc surface because it is easily damaged. Over the years, floppy discs have come in different sizes (e.g. 3", 3.5", 5.25" or 8" diameters) although by far the most common today is 3.5". In reality floppy discs are being used less and less often both due to limitations of their storage capacity and the advent of alternatives such as memory sticks (see below).

The hard disc and drive

Hard disc drives contain one or more rigid discs made from ceramic or aluminium coated with magnetic material. They may be sealed into the disc drive unit – this protects them from dirt and careless handling (but they must not be dropped, as this can damage them). Hard discs are often built into the computer.

Removable single hard disc systems are available, typically storing 20 Gb or more. Modern desktop systems are typically sold with 60 Gb or more.

CD-ROM

There are other backing storage media now in use which are non-magnetic, such as compact discs (often referred to as CD-ROM and are read-only). There are also recordable CDs (CD-R) and rewritable CDs (CD-RW). The CD medium stores up to 700 Mb.

DVD-ROM

Recently the DVD-ROM (Digital Versatile Disc) is replacing the CD due to its huge memory capacity and the very high quality of stored images. Whole movies can easily be stored on DVD allowing the viewer options over video such as choice of language, skip to scene etc. The DVD medium is capable of storing 4.7 Gb.

Zip Disc (or Jaz drive)

Zip discs are similar to floppy discs since the individual discs are removable, but they hold much larger quantities of data than conventional floppy discs – usually between 100 Mb and 2 Gb.

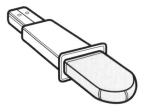

USB Memory Stick or pen drive

Memory sticks are solid-state memory devices. They are approximately the size of a pen and they easily fit into a pocket. To use them you simply plug them into the USB port of any computer. They are very light and very portable. Since they work with PC or Mac they are an effective way of transferring files between the two. Typical size is 32 Mb-1 Gb.

The table below gives a comparison of different backing store media.

	Speed (Kb/s)	Cost	Capacity
Floppy	36	A few pence	1.44 Mb
Hard drive	1000	Usually built in to computer (£50 upwards for extra drives)	Up to 500 Gb
Zip	Between floppy and hard drive	Discs around £20 but a zip drive has to be bought too. These are under £80	100 Mb-2 Gb
CD	Up to 720	Less than £1 each for CD-R: slightly more for CD-R/W	700 Mb
DVD	Similar to CD	Less than £1 each: slightly more for erasable.	4.7 Gb
Memory Stick	480	£25 upwards	256 Mb-8 Gb

Backing Storage requirements

These vary from application to application. Small files will fit on anything from a floppy disc upwards. Larger files such as Video or sound clips are too big for a floppy and need to be saved on a hard drive, CD, Memory stick etc. Before being run they are best copied over to the hard drive since the access time is quicker than say a CD.

Input devices

These input information into the processor.

Keyboard

Keyboards are used to enter text and numbers. They are usually standard QWERTY-type but not always.

Mouse

The mouse is very important in WIMP systems, used to move a pointer around the screen and make selections by pressing a button.

Trackball

The trackball does the same things as a mouse. It is used to move a pointer around the screen and make selections by pressing a button.

Scanner

The hand scanner is moved by hand to input graphic data. Flat-bed scanners move automatically to scan images.

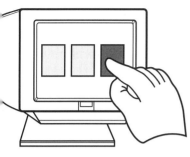

Touch-sensitive screen

A touch-sensitive screen registers where the user touches it. If the software places a menu on the screen, then the option is chosen by touching the choice on the screen either with a stylus or with their finger.

Joystick

A joystick is used to control objects on a computer screen. It is frequently used for games and sometimes used instead of a mouse.

Touchpad

Laptops and palmtops often use a touchpad instead of a mouse. The touchpad is a small touch-sensitive pad usually about 3 cm square built into the computer.

Graphics tablet

Graphics tablets use a special pen (a stylus) which is pressed against a pressure-sensitive surface. The position of the stylus on the surface is registered by the computer.

Microphone

A microphone is used to talk or sing into to convert sound into electrical signals which the computer can use. They can also help make use of the Internet as an alternative to a telephone system.

Cameras

A digital camera is now replacing a traditional camera for many people. The advantage is it uses no film so needs no developing. Firms such as Kodak now offer to print out digital photos from CD. This is ideal if pictures are to be used on a computer since they may be loaded straight in. Some of the latest also record short video sequences.

Many people now choose to edit their own home movies by using a digital video camera and editing software in the computer. The software often comes free with some manufacturers machines. Again it loads straight into the computer and can be edited easily.

Webcams are small (usually cheap) cameras that sit on top of the computer and broadcasts pictures to the Internet. If used with broadband access these can give 24 hour viewing and thus can be used for security purposes.

Voice recognition

The input device is a microphone but it is the computer software which allows the voice to be recognised and the commands understood. The system is taught to recognise simple commands by the user repeating them several times into the microphone.

Handwriting recognition

Some of the latest devices recognise handwriting. The user writes on a type of graphics tablet and the computer software can recognise the handwriting. To help this process, the system learns the writing by the user entering sample characters. These devices are often hand-held units.

Specialised input devices

Other specialised input devices exist, tailored to the needs of the user. For example, disabled users may use special keyboards, blowpipes or movement detectors.

Output devices

Output devices receive information from the processor and present it in a suitable form.

Laser printer

In a laser printer, a laser beam charges a sensitive drum. This picks up toner powder which is transferred to the paper, giving high quality text and graphics. One full page is printed at a time making them fast. The toner cartridges also last a long time (up to 15 000 pages) making them good for long print runs.

Inkjet printer

In an inkjet printer, the characters are formed by rapidly firing small bubbles of ink at the paper. An alternative name is a bubble-jet printer. This type of printer gives very good quality output. Some portable printers are inkjets.

Comparison of printers

It is difficult to compare lasers against ink jets since both types have a huge variety of models and specifications but the table below gives some idea.

	Laser	Ink Jet
Speed (pages per minute)	6-30	4 -18 B/W and 2-14 colour
Cost	£100 - £2000 +	£40 - £2500
Running costs	Tend to be lower than ink-jets since although toner cartridges are more expensive (£30 - £100 +) they last a long time.	Fairly expensive to run as most need two cartridges (one black and one colour) which cost £25 -£30 and don't last long with heavy usage.
Resolution (dpi)	600 - 2400	300 - 600

Flat-bed plotter

A flat-bed plotter is a type of printer in which the pen carriage moves up and down and from side to side. This allows line graphics to be drawn.

Monitor (Visual Display Unit)

Operating in a similar way to a TV screen, a monitor gives a picture made from many pixels on the screen.

Loudspeaker

A loudspeaker allows sound and speech output to be produced.

LCD (Liquid Crystal Display)

Liquid Crystal Displays are low power devices often used by portable battery-powered systems. A very small current causes pixels to be turned on, so producing graphics. The LCD device can be in the form of a VDU (which is complex and therefore expensive) or can use preformed characters (for example, digital watches and calculator and CD tuner displays).

TFT(Thin Film Transistor) or Flat screen monitor

TFT screens are high performance monitors which use series of LCDS with transistors built into every pixel within the screen.

Specialised output devices

Other specialised output devices exist which are tailored to the needs of the user. For example, virtual reality requires special display screens (often mounted in a headset).

Sound card

Computers used for music or other applications where sound is important can have their output enhanced by adding a sound card. This sits in a slot in the PC tower and if connected to a good pair of speakers can result in very high quality sound output.

Graphics card

Computers used for applications requiring high quality graphics such as games playing can have their output enhanced by adding a high specification graphics card. This sits in a slot in the PC tower and if connected to a good quality monitor can result in very high quality picture output.

Questions

3.19   Name four types of computer and give a typical user for each.

3.20   a)   Give two differences between ROM and RAM.

       b)   Name two different types of magnetic media.

       c)   Describe two precautions to be taken when using magnetic media.

3.21   a)   Name four different input devices.

       b)   Name four different output devices.

       c)   Name two different types of printer and compare these in terms of speed, cost and quality.

3.22   a)   Name four types of backing store and give a typical use for each.

       b)   For each device you chose above, give an indication of cost and capacity.

3.23   Name one backing storage device that does not use magnetic media and give the typical storage capacity of the media it uses.

3.24   a)   *Name one specialised input device and suggest who might use it.*

       b)   *Name one specialised output device.*

3.25   An advertisement for a new computer system describes it as a multimedia system. Describe the typical hardware which you would expect such a system to have and why it is needed.

Answers to Revision Questions

Congratulations – you have now reached the end of these revision notes. If you have studied every page carefully and learnt the contents you have made good progress in preparing yourself for your Standard Grade Computing examinations.

Good luck!

CHAPTER 1: GENERAL PURPOSE PACKAGES

Need for GPPs

1.1   Three tasks which people wanted a computer to do in the 1980s were:

- typing in and editing data
- doing calculations with data
- presenting information as graphs and pictures.

1.2   a) A database stores information in an organised way, which makes it easy to retrieve.

      b) A word-processor stores text and can bring together information from other general purpose packages.

      c) A spreadsheet processes figures and produces accounts. It can also display charts and graphs using the spreadsheet information.

1.3.   To send the information electronically from office to office requires extra hardware (a modem and access to telephone lines) and software (communications software).

Common Features

1.4   a) The process Open will load a document which has been saved on backing store.

      b) The process Print part prints only a part of the document, such as a single page or a selected area.

      c) The process Amend data alters some data in the document, such as making the line length larger or changing the spelling of a word.

      d) The process Copy data copies the data that has been marked in some way. It is then ready to be pasted somewhere else.

      e) The process Move data takes the data that has been selected and moves it to another place in the document.

1.5   The font can be changed. This gives the characters a different shape. The character size can be changed to make the text smaller or larger. The style of the text can be changed to make it bold or underlined.

1.6   a) The process of regularly making copies is called backup.

      b) It is important to make backup copies because the original file could be lost or damaged. This could happen accidentally or it might be deliberate.

1.7   A printer driver is software which is selected by the user. This allows different printers to work properly with a particular computer by selecting the appropriate printer driver.

1.8   A header is placed at the top of every page in the document and may contain text or graphics. The information will be mainly the same on each page, although automatic page numbering can be set to give a different page number on each page. A footer is similar to a header except it appears at the bottom of a page.

1.9   Numeric, textual, graphic, audio, photographic, animation, video.

Human Computer Interface

1.10   a)   The Human Computer Interface controls how the computer system appears to the user as the user interacts with it to change data and control programs.

        b)   Examples of features of the Human Computer Interface that the user can alter are the size of a window and the colour in which text is displayed.

1.11   A user-friendly Human Computer Interface is one which is easy to use. This means that the user can easily understand what to do and what is happening with the computer system.

1.12   a)   Menu-driven is more user-friendly.

        b)   Command-driven is usually preferred by experienced users.

        c)   In a command-driven program the user selects what to do next by typing in a command in a special language.

        d)   In a menu-driven program the user selects what to do by making a selection from a menu printed on the screen by the computer. This may involve typing a letter or number or using a mouse to indicate the required option.

1.13   a)   WIMP stands for Windows, Icons, Mouse and Pull-down menu (alternatively Windows, Icons, Menus and Pointers).

        b)   An alternative name for a WIMP interface is a Graphical User Interface (or GUI).

        c)   In a WIMP system the keyboard is used to enter text and numbers.

1.14   a)   An icon is a small picture on the screen used to represent items which can be selected or used.

        b)   Two examples of icons are the wastebasket and a floppy disc:

blank

Wastebasket

        c)   The user could select an icon by moving the mouse until the pointer is pointing at the icon, then pressing the mouse button to highlight the icon.

1.15   An online tutorial takes you stage by stage through the different features of the program. Online help can be accessed while the program is running. It is usually arranged in help menus, which allow the user to choose the part of the program for which help is needed.

Word-processing

1.16   The term enter means to type in text.

       The term amend means to alter text already present.

       The term delete means to remove text.

       The term save means to send a copy to Backing Store (disc).

       The term print is to make a paper copy.

       The term retrieve means to load back into the computer the text that has been saved on backing store.

1.17 Wordwrap is the process that occurs when a word is typed in towards the end of a line. If the word is too long to fit into the space available, the whole word is moved to the start of the next line. It is often used by word-processors to avoid words being split between two lines.

1.18 a) Tabulation uses preset positions along a line. The cursor is moved to these positions by pressing the TAB key.

b) Typical TAB settings are every 1.27 cm or half inch.

c) The cursor often looks like a flashing line in the text.

1.19 a) So that the name and address appear on the right-hand side of the page.

b) Normal text in a book is usually set up to be left justified with the text lined up on the left-hand side of the page.

c) Newspaper columns are usually fully justified so that both left- and right-hand sides are lined up.

1.20 a) The words known by the system are usually kept in a separate file called a dictionary.

b) A typical system knows about 50 000 words.

c) The system would probably not know names of people or towns.

d) The system can learn new words by adding them to its dictionary file.

1.21 a) A standard paragraph is used many times to make different letters.

b) Standard paragraphs can be used when the same text is used in many different documents, such as a company giving details on a delayed order.

1.22 a) A standard letter is one which is sent to many people with only a few details changed, such as names and addresses.

b) A standard letter file may be linked to a database file.

c) The process is mail merge.

Spreadsheets

1.23 A typical spreadsheet is a table or grid made up of cells which are named from the column and rows which they occupy.

1.24 The three types of information that a spreadsheet can contain are numbers, text and formulas. For example: 23, total, =A2+B3

1.25 Data in spreadsheets can be used to produce bar charts, pie charts and line charts.

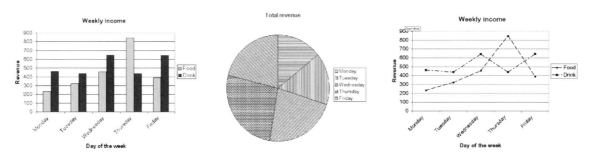

1.26 a) Automatic calculation causes the spreadsheet to recalculate all the values in formulas every time a new value or formula is entered. With manual calculation the recalculation is only done when an instruction is given to the spreadsheet to do it.

b) It would be preferable to use manual calculation if large numbers of formulas or values are to be entered or changed. This would allow quicker entry of the new data without time being taken to calculate after each one was entered.

c) The default option is usually automatic calculation.

1.27 Replication is the process where the contents of one cell are copied to other cells, adjusting for the column and row references in any formulas used.

	A	B	C
1			=A1+B1
2			=A2+B2
3			=A3+B3
4			=A4+B4
5			=A5+B5
6			=A6+B6
7			=A7+B7
8			=A8+B8
9			
10			
11			

1.28   a) Cell attributes refers to the options for the display of data in cells in different ways. For example, the number 2.987 could be displayed as 2.987, 3, 2.99 or £2.98 depending on the attributes chosen.

        b) The date could be displayed as 1/1/00 or January 1, 2000.

1.29   a) AVERAGE () returns one number which is the average of the range given in the brackets e.g. if the cells given contained 4,5,6 then average would be 5.

        b) MINIMUM() returns the smallest number in the given range.

        c) MAXIMUM() returns the largest number in the given range

1.30   a) Information should be locked in cells where the data is not to be changed by the user, for example text for headings or fixed values and formulas.

        b) It is desirable to lock these cells so that the user cannot accidentally change their contents.

1.31   Cell B1 will have the value 0 if the contents of cell A1 are greater than 31. If this is not so (A1 contents are 31 or less) then B1 will contain the value 1.

1.32   a) Relative replication of cells causes the column and row references in formulas to change according to the row and column into which the cell is copied. For example, if cell C1 contains the formula =A1*B1 and this is copied relatively into cell C2, the new formula would be =A2*B2.

          The same process carried out using absolute replication would result in cell C2 containing the same formula as that in cell C1, that is =A1*B1.

        b) A dollar sign is often placed in front of the row or column reference to make it absolute, for example $A$1*$B$1.

        c) A user may wish to make a cell reference absolute when a fixed cell is always to be referred to in a formula, for example the rate of VAT for all VAT calculations.

Databases

1.33   A file is the complete set of data stored on disc. A record is the data for one person – their name, date of birth and favourite colour. A field is one of the separate pieces of information for one person – their date of birth, for example.

1.34   A file is searched to find those records which match what is being looked for. A simple search checks for the contents of only one field. A complex search uses at least two fields.

1.35   a) The way in which a particular file is displayed is called the format or layout.

        b) Common formats are card format and list format.

1.36   a) A computed field is one where the contents have been calculated using a formula, usually using the contents of other fields in the calculation.

        b) By changing the input format, data entry can be made simpler, for example by matching the data entry to that on a form containing the data.

        c) The output format can display the output in different ways, not necessarily showing all the fields. So, the fields may be shown in a different order and position.

1.37   a) The order of all the records is changed, placing them in the order determined by the way in which they are sorted on the selected field.

        b) This allows two sorts to be done in one operation. For example, sorting a list of names into alphabetical order of surname and forename.

Graphics

1.38   a) Three examples of tools in a graphics program are line, circle and rectangle drawing tools.

        b) Tool attributes are the properties of the object, i.e. how the object appears.

        c) Two examples are changing the thickness of a line and the fill pattern of a circle.

        d) When a graphic is scaled, it is made larger or smaller.

Expert Systems

1.39   a) An Expert System is a computerised databank which can imitate some of the functions of a human expert in a small area of expertise. It answers questions using facts and rules entered into the knowledge base.

        b) Two areas are (any from): giving legal advice (helping lawyers), medical diagnosis (helping doctors), car diagnosis (helping mechanics).

Electronic Communication and Networks

1.40   a) A network is a set of computers and peripherals joined together by cables. This allows expensive peripherals to be used by more than one computer. This keeps costs down, while making the peripherals available to all the computers. It also allows files to be shared.

        b) Local Area Networks (LANs) and Wide Area Networks (WANs). LANs operate over fairly small distances, typically a room or building, use simple and inexpensive cabling and have few transmission errors. WANs operate over large distances, e.g. between towns or countries, use more expensive cabling and commonly have more frequent transmission errors.

1.41   a) Electronic mail requires a computer system, communications software, a modem and access to telephone lines. A subscription to an e-mail service is also required.

        b) An electronic mailbox is an area of a computer's memory where messages can be left for other users to read by making a connection to the system.

        c) One advantage is that a message can be sent to many people in one operation. A disadvantage is that the correct equipment is required.

1.42   Netiquette means the agreed standards of behaviour used in an online environment such as emails and discussion boards TYPING IN BLOCK CAPITALS is considered shouting and would be 'bad netiquette'.

1.43   a) In a multi-access system many users have a terminal which is connected to a mainframe computer. The terminal is a keyboard and screen which is using the processing power of the mainframe computer.

        b) A remote terminal is located some distance from the mainframe computer and uses modems to connect to the mainframe.

        c) Time slicing occurs when each user is allocated a short period of time in turn to be connected to the mainframe. Because the mainframe computer operates very quickly, each user appears to have sole use of the mainframe.

Internet

1.44   Shopping, banking, airline booking, car hire, holidays …

1.45   Browser

1.46   Hypertext is the language used to write web pages. It allows links to other web pages.

1.47   Google, Ask Jeeves, Yahoo etc.

1.48   a) Online means a device is connected to, and communicating with, the computer.

        b) Because phone connection time costs money, it is more economical to prepare documents off-line, therefore not using phone time to type in the information.

1.49   Freeware is totally free for anyone to use. Shareware is free to sample but a small fee is payable for continued usage. Commercial software – full price must be paid to obtain it

Desktop Publishing

1.50   a) A template is a pre-written outline or structure of a file available for the user to adapt to suit themselves.

        b) A wizard is a piece of software that takes the user step-by-step through a process usually used to install new software or for a process such as mail merge.

1.51   Clip Art means a selection of graphics or sound bytes available for insertion into other packages.

1.52   a) Importing a graphic means to take a graphic into a program from another source (the WWW or another package).

        b) Scaling means resizing.

Presentation and Multimedia

1.53   Multimedia means a mixture of text, graphics and sound to present information. Often large files are used and CDs/DVDs are required for storage.

1.54   PowerPoint would be used to create a presentation slide show for accompanying a talk.

1.55   Presentations can contain text, graphics, sounds, web links, video clips.

1.56   A hyperlink is used to access a page on the WWW.

Web Page Creation

1.57   Web pages can be created using HTML or an authoring package such as Front Page.

1.58   Pages can contain graphics, text, links, video.

1.59   a) A hotspot changes as a mouse hovers over it.

        b) A hyperlink, usually blue and underlined, links to another web page when clicked.

Integration

1.60   a) Typical multi-task operations are the creation of charts from spreadsheet data and the ability to draw simple shapes in a word-processor.

        b) Pull-down menus in all parts of the integrated package are similar and key combinations for common tasks such as printing a document are the same.

1.61   If the link is static then it exists only as long as the data is being transferred from the spreadsheet to the chart. Once this has taken place, the link is broken. Further changes to the spreadsheet data will not appear as changes to the chart. If the link is dynamic then it is not broken after transfer and further changes to the spreadsheet data will cause the chart to show the new values.

Implications

1.62   a) Page layout by compositors is now done electronically using desktop publishing software. Typists have now become word-processor operators.

        b) Large numbers of names and addresses are taken from a database and used for labels on envelopes to send material to many people.

1.63   a) Companies can protect data stored on computer by keeping computer room doors locked, by requiring a password to gain access to important files and by keeping backup copies of vital information in fireproof safes.

        b) A computer hacker is someone who tries to gain access to a computer system when they do not have permission for access.

1.64   a) Setting up costs for businesses include the cost of the hardware (e.g. computer systems and printers) and software costs (e.g. programs and application packages).

        b) Running costs for business computers include equipment repairs and cost of consumables (e.g. paper, toner and discs).

1.65   a)   The Data Protection Act (1984) requires companies to register if they wish to hold data about more than a few people. It only allows data to be stored for lawful purposes. People have the right to check the accuracy of data stored about them (with some exceptions, such as police files).

            b)   A data user is someone who has, or controls, personal data about other people.

CHAPTER 2: INDUSTRIAL AND COMMERCIAL APPLICATIONS

Automated Systems

2.1   a)   Benefits to companies which use automated systems include: tasks can be carried out more quickly; high accuracy of manufacture; tasks can be done in hot or cold conditions where humans cannot work; greater efficiency, as more goods can be produced for less cost.

     b)   An interface is used to allow for differences in the speed of different devices, and for differences in the devices' codes for handling data.

2.2   An analogue signal has a wide range of values which are constantly changing. A digital signal can only be one of two values (0 or 1).

 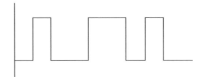

2.3   a)   A sensor detects events such as heat and light level changing. It is an INPUT device.

     b)   Three sensors are a heat sensor, a light sensor and a movement sensor.

2.4.   Three output devices used with automated systems are a heater, a motor and a lamp.

2.5   a)   Feedback occurs when information is returned to the CPU from a device controlled by a computer.

     b)   Feedback is provided by sensors placed on the output device.

2.6   Automated systems which are adaptable can be easily reprogrammed to do different tasks.

2.7   An A-to-D converter converts analogue signals to digital signals. It is used for input. A D-to-A converter converts digital information to analogue. It is an output device.

2.8   a)   A robot is a machine, controlled by a computer, which is flexible. It can be made to do more than one task by reprogramming it.

     b)   A robot is not shaped like a human because the robot might overbalance as the body is top heavy; it is difficult to make robots walk like humans and the size and shape might be unsuitable for the task to be done.

2.9   Please see diagram:

2.10 a) A robot in a fixed position is a stationary robot.

b) Mobile robots usually use wheels or tracks to move about.

2.11 a) A wire is buried in the ground. When an electric current is passed through the wire, a magnetic field is generated. Sensors on the mobile robot sense this and so can follow the wire.

b) A white-line follower.

2.12 CAD/CAM stands for Computer Aided Design/Computer Aided Manufacture. The computer is used both in the design process and manufacture, with details of the design being passed on to the manufacturing process.

2.13 Robots can be programmed using a program which tells them exactly what to do. Robots can also be programmed by the 'lead-through' method where a human operator, connected to sensors, shows the computer what to do.

2.14 a) A high level language is often best for the programmer to use.

b) It is easy for the programmer to make changes and correct any errors in the program.

2.15 a) Computer simulation is suitable: for practising defusing bombs which is dangerous; for learning to fly aeroplanes which is expensive and for learning to control nuclear power stations which is also dangerous.

b) Movement in simulators may be made by hydraulic systems and visual effects can be provided on large screens.

2.16 a) Real-time processes use the computer to process events as they occur. What the computer does next depends on what has just happened.

b) An example of a real-time process is in an automated factory. There must be an immediate response if a breakdown occurs.

2.17 a) Employees might worry that they will not be able to understand the new machines and so lose their jobs, or that they will find it difficult to learn new skills.

b) Employees will have better working conditions and more leisure time.

c) Running costs in automated factories are lower because fewer workers are required; areas where only machines work do not need the same levels of light or heat that humans require; the only costs are the repair and maintenance of equipment.

2.18 a) Special control languages were developed for automated systems because some of the instructions the operator needs to use are specific to the needs of the machines.

b) The specialised programs might be stored in customised ROM.

Commercial Data Processing

2.19 a) Companies use computers for data processing because there is a very large amount to be processed daily, computers are very fast at the processing and they process the data accurately.

b) The main stages in the data processing cycle are data collection, data preparation, data input, data processing, storage of data and output of data.

2.20 a) Data is any information that can be stored in a computer and can be meaningless without further explanation. Information is data in a form that humans can understand.

b) An example of data is a simple number like 12 345. This could mean almost anything. When it is put into context it is meaningful, such as cost of new car = £12 345.

2.21 a) Bar codes, magnetic ink character recognition, mark sense cards and magnetic stripes are methods of data collection designed to eliminate operator errors.

b) Bar codes are used on books, magnetic ink characters are used on cheques for the automatic reading of account details, mark sense cards are used for stock control and recording examination answers, and magnetic stripes are used on cheque cards.

2.22 a) A check digit is an extra digit added to numerical data to check that the data has been entered correctly into the computer. The original digit is calculated from the other numbers. The computer then recalculates the check digit and compares the result with the value entered.

b) Check digits are used in ISBN numbers and credit card numbers.

c) The characters used for check digits are usually the numbers 0 to 9 and the letter X.

d) Two other checks on the data entered are range checks and length checks.

 2.23 a) Optical Character Recognition reads characters on paper and inputs the data into a computer.

b) The font and size of characters are important.

c) Reading documents to save having to retype them into the computer; reading the line of reference numbers printed on some electricity bills.

2.24 a) Interactive processing has a program running all the time and processes data immediately. The result of this processing affects the next action of the computer.

b) Interactive processing is used for operating bank accounts.

2.25 a) Validation of data checks to see if the data is within prescribed limits, such as the days in a month in the range 1 to 31.

b) Double entry requires the same data to be entered by two different operators.

c) Verification

2.26 a) Magnetic tape stores data by sequential access.

b) Magnetic disc stores data by direct access.

c) Sequential access is also called serial access; direct access is also called random access.

d) Sequential access files are typically used for backup purposes.

2.27 A mainframe computer would be required; many terminals would be connected, together with several high speed printers, magnetic tape and magnetic disc backing storage devices.

2.28 a) A programmer writes programs and modifies existing programs. An engineer maintains and repairs computer systems. A network manager has overall responsibility to maintain a Local Area Network usually within one company.

b) One other job is a systems analyst.

2.29 a) Initial costs include computers, printers, backing storage, software, buildings, furniture and telephone systems.

b) Running costs include salaries, staff training, electricity, consumables, repairs and rentals.

2.30 a) A point-of-sale terminal is programmed with the prices of all the items in the shop. It can scan each item and automatically give the price.

b) There is little chance of pricing mistakes.

c) Electronic funds transfer does not use notes or coins. Instead, the customer's account at the bank has funds removed and transferred to the business's account by computer.

2.31 a) At a later stage the file will be processed by the computer.

b) The file may be a print spool file or a partially processed file.

2.32 Information is stolen to find out about prices so that a lower bid could be made for a job. Deliberate destruction of data could put a competitor out of business.

2.33 a) The user types in the password when asked. The password does not appear on the screen. If the password is correct then the user gains access to the system.

b) Different passwords and user names give access to different types of data and files (different levels of access).

c) One other method could be to keep the building secure (keeping doors locked), only allowing access to people who work there.

2.34 The company will buy lists of people who are suited to its purposes, for example people living in a certain part of the country or with particular interests.

2.35 In the manual system, data is entered on large amounts of paper which have to be stored and kept in order. This requires many staff. In the computerised system, less staff are required with much less paper because the files are on backing storage.

CHAPTER 3: SYSTEMS: SOFTWARE AND HARDWARE

Systems Software

3.1   a)   High-level languages use English words to give instructions to a computer. One high-level language instruction represents several machine code instructions. The instructions are carried out in sequence. Most have commands for process, repetition and decisions. High-level languages are designed to solve problems.

       b)   Translation is the process of turning a high-level language program into machine code.

3.2   a)   Source code is the text program written on a word-processor. When this is compiled, it produces the object code. It is the object code which is executed when the program is run.

       b)   A programmer must go to the source code, make the changes, then compile the program again to produce new object code.

       c)   A compiled program is already in machine code and ready to be executed. An interpreted program has to be translated as each line is met, and then executed. The translation takes time and so the program runs more slowly.

Operating and Filing Systems

3.3   a)   An operating system is a set of programs which gives instructions to the computer. It takes control when the computer is first switched on.

       b)   Four functions are memory management, file management, input/output control and scheduling of jobs.

       c)   If stored in RAM, the operating system can easily be changed and updated.

3.4   a)   Data files contain the data used by programs. Program files contain the instructions that tell the computer what to do.

       b)   An example of a data file is the text file produced by a word-processing program. An example of a program file is the word-processing program itself.

       c)   A directory on a disc contains information about the files on the disc, their names and where they are kept on the disc.

3.5   a)   Background tasks are suited to interactive systems because there are always times when the processor is otherwise idle, waiting for something to happen. It is at these times the processor can perform background tasks until the main program requires the processor again.

       b)   One example is background printing. Data can be sent to the printer whenever the main application is not using the processor.

Low Level Machine

3.6   A bit is a binary digit (a 1 or a 0). A byte is a group of eight bits. A kilobyte is approximately 1000 bytes (exactly 1024 bytes). A megabyte is approximately 1000 kilobytes (exactly 1024 kilobytes). A gigabyte is approximately 1000 megabytes (exactly 1024 megabytes). A terabyte is 1000 gigabytes.

3.7   a)

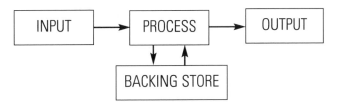

b) The processor and main memory are the two main parts of the CPU.

3.8 a) The machine code does not have to be translated before being executed and so runs faster than a high-level language.

b) Machine code is difficult for humans to understand and errors are difficult to detect and correct.

3.9 a) The place values are as shown here:

place value	8	4	2	1
binary value	1	1	1	0

so the decimal equivalent is: $1\times8 + 1\times4 + 1\times2 + 0\times1 = 14$

b) The place values are: 128, 64, 32, 16, 8, 4, 2, 1.

3.10 a) ASCII stands for American Standard Code for Information Interchange.

b) ASCII code 65 represents the character A.

c) One byte is required to store each character.

3.11 a) In computing terms, a word is a collection of bits treated as a single unit by the processor. This is usually the number of bits moved as a group, typically 8, 16 or 32 bits.

b) Addressability relates to the number of unique storage locations that the processor can normally use.

3.12 a) A pixel is a picture element, the smallest element of a graphic. It can be on or off to turn the colour on or off.

b) The greater the number of pixels used to show a graphic of a given size, the higher the resolution.

3.13 a) A character set is the group of characters represented by a range of ASCII codes.

b) With different character sets, the same ASCII code might represent different characters. For example, in one set a code may be the character D and in another set it might represent the character Δ.

3.14 Two examples of the function of control characters include moving the cursor back one space and clearing the screen.

3.15 a) An integer number is a whole number.

b) The range of binary integer numbers which can be stored in eight bits is from 00000000 to 11111111.

c) As decimal numbers the range is from 0 to 255.

3.16 a) When numbers are stored as mantissa and exponent this is called floating point format.

b) An example of a binary number stored in floating point format is:

$$1001011010010110 \times 2^{10010110}$$

The mantissa is the number 1001011010010110

and the exponent is the number 10010110.

3.17 a) The control unit supervises the decoding and execution of program instructions. Operations inside the processor and flow of data between memory and processor are involved.

b) A typical logic operation in the ALU is an AND operation.

c) Registers are fast access storage areas within the CPU.

3.18 The total number of pixels needed is height × width. As one bit is needed per pixel this is also the number of bits. Dividing by 8 gives the number of bytes. For a display 800 × 600:

Number of bits = 800 × 600 = 480000 bits.

Number of bytes = 480000 / 8 = 60000 bytes = 60 Kb.

Hardware

3.19   Mainframe   large company such as mail order

         Desktop   home user or office worker

         Laptop   portable user i.e. student, rep

         Palmtop   smallest portable again student or sales rep

3.20   a)   ROM contents can only be read and they cannot be changed. The contents are permanent, so when the computer is switched off, they are not lost. RAM contents can be read and altered. The contents are not permanent, and when the computer is switched off, they are lost.

         b)   Two types of magnetic media are tapes and discs.

         c)   Two precautions to be taken with magnetic media are not to touch the media surface and to keep the media away from dirt.

3.21   a)   Four examples of input devices are a keyboard, a mouse, a scanner and a light pen.

         b)   Four examples of output devices are a printer, a plotter, a monitor and a loudspeaker.

         c)   Laser and ink jet. Laser better quality costs now getting closer although laser slightly more expensive (£100+ as opposed to £40+). Running costs for laser cheaper in the long run.

3.22   a) + b)   Floppy disc- storage of portable personal files, costs pence, stores 1 Mb;

                 Hard drive – main storage on desktop for files and applications, costs £40+, stores 40 Mb upwards;

                 CD – installation discs for new packages, multimedia presentations, costs 50p, stores 700 Mb;

                 Memory stick – computer back-up or file transfer, costs £25-150, stores 32 Mb-1 Gb.

3.23   A backing storage device that is not magnetic is an optical disc drive. Its typical capacity is 128 Mb.

3.24   a)   An example of a specialised input device is a blowpipe. It might be used by a disabled person.

         b)   An example of a specialised output device is a virtual reality helmet.

3.25   A multimedia system will use a variety of hardware. This may include CD-ROM players and laser disc players because CD-ROMS and laser discs can store large amounts of data. Suitable output devices will be needed, such as high resolution monitors and high quality sound reproduction systems.

Index